KU-547-917

This annual belongs to:

....

Editor: Nick Clark
Written by: Martin Ross
Design by: Darren Miles
Contributors: Caroline Dunk & Eddie Jones

Managing Director: Mike Riddell
Managing Editor: Alan O'Keefe
Head of Production: Mark Irvine

All photographic imagery supplied by Getty/PA Photos/The FA

Statistical information supplied by The Press Association Ltd.

The final cut-off date for compiling this annual was Monday June 1st 2015 (unless otherwise specified within). All reasonable efforts have been made to ensure the statistical information and biographical details were accurate at that time. Any subsequent player transfers and/or managerial changes after the above date are unfortunately beyond our control. All statistics are based on full England career to the cut-off date unless stated on page that data relates to the period from the start of the 2014 World Cup onwards.

FSC
www.fsc.org
MIX
Paper from
responsible sources
FSC® C005461

© 2015. Published by Panini UK Ltd.

© The Football Association Ltd 2015. The FA brand mark and The FA England brand mark are official trademarks of The Football Association Ltd and are the subject of extensive trademark registrations worldwide. Manufactured under licence by Panini UK Ltd. Made in the EU.

ISBN: 978-1-846532-18-4

£7.99

TOGETHER FOR
ENGLAND

Every England match is an exciting occasion for all proud England supporters. From the moment when the team walks out on the lush Wembley turf to the roar of the crowd to the nail-biting final minutes of a vital match, it's a real rollercoaster ride! But can you imagine how it actually feels to pull on that famous three lions shirt? It must be amazing! That's why in this annual, we've tried to give you a real behind-the-scenes taste of what it's like to be part of the England set-up. We take a close look at your favourite England stars, meet Roy Hodgson and his team, check out the world class facilities the team play and train in and there are loads of fun features for you to enjoy too!

Whether you watch England from the comfort of your sofa or are lucky enough to actually be in the stadium, we really hope you'll enjoy the Official England Annual 2016!

Thank you for being an England fan!

ENGERRR–LAANNND!

CONTENTS

ST GEORGE'S PARK

PLUS
WIN!

WELCOME TO
WEMBLEY!

England's home, Wembley Stadium, is one of the most famous sporting venues in the world and is a fascinating place to visit even when there isn't a match on. The atmosphere is incredible. But if you can't get there, why not take our tour, walk where the England legends have walked before you and get a real behind-the-scenes peek at the great stadium. This is the inside track!

DID YOU KNOW?

The arch is **133 metres tall** and has a width of 7.4 metres so an access cart can be driven through it to look after it. At the top, there is a warning beacon for low-flying aircraft on their way to Heathrow and Gatwick airports.

1

Wembley was designed by The World Stadium Team, a joint partnership between HOK Sport Architecture and Foster and Partners.

6

THE STEPS AND ROYAL BOX

If you've won a trophy, going up the famous Wembley steps to collect your medal from the Royal Box is an amazing moment. There are **107** steps up to the Royal Box, which contains 400 seats for the VIPs!

DID YOU KNOW?

BOBBY MOORE PLAYED FOR ENGLAND **108 TIMES** AND CAPTAINED THE TEAM **90 TIMES**, INCLUDING WHEN ENGLAND WON THE WORLD CUP 50 YEARS AGO!

BOBBY MOORE STATUE

Outside the entrance to the stadium, you are instantly reminded of England's 1966 World Cup victory at the old Wembley by the statue of England captain, Bobby Moore.

3

10

11

As you head for Wembley up Olympic Way, you will gasp at the sheer size of the gleaming stadium, but what will really catch your eye is the iconic arch that reaches for the sky high above the pitch. At 315m, the arch is the longest single-span roof structure in the world.

OLYMPIC WAY

THE PRESS ROOM

The Wembley Press Room has 196 seats and is the largest in the UK. This is where Roy Hodgson and Wayne Rooney, plus England's Man of the Match, talk to the newspapers, television and radio reporters about how they won the game! Actually they have to appear, win, lose or draw but it's always easier after a win!

WEMBLEY FACT FILE

Name: Wembley Stadium

Address: Wembley, London HA9 0WS

Opened: 19 May 2007

Capacity: 90,000

First England Game: 01/06/2007 England 1 Brazil 1

THE PITCH

As you gaze across the beautiful green turf of the Wembley pitch, you can't help but dream of playing on it. And who knows, one day you might! At 105 metres long and 68 metres wide, it is one of the largest pitches in the country.

THE ROOF

The Wembley roof is **11 acres** in size with four moveable acres, when it is closed it covers every seat but not the pitch!

DID YOU KNOW?

The Wembley pitch is 97% natural grass and 3% artificial Desso fibres, which provides a top class playing surface all year round.

DESSO FIBRES   GRASS

THE CORPORATE BOXES

The corporate boxes at Wembley can be adapted for special occasions. One lucky family won the chance to sleep over at Wembley before the 2014 FA Cup Final. The windows in these boxes are specially designed so sound bounces off them and echoes around the stadium to create even more atmosphere!

SOUND   SOUND   SOUND

There are **2,618** toilets in Wembley Stadium, more than any other building in the world. There are also **98** kitchens and **nine** restaurants!

THE STAGE POCKET

The seats in the stage pocket are retractable and allow room for stages to be built for concerts.

DRESSING ROOMS

Now you're really on the inside! This is where the England stars get ready with the distant sound of the crowd in their ears and their nerves kicking in. There are four identical dressing rooms at Wembley, England always use Dressing Room 1 and their opponents use Dressing Room 2.

8 IT TAKES **EIGHT HOURS** TO PREPARE THE ENGLAND KIT BEFORE EACH GAME.

1. The arch
2. The roof
3. The 107 steps
4. Commentary box
5. TV studios
6. Scoreboards
7. The Players' Tunnel
8. Corporate boxes
9. Seating
10. The Bobby Moore Seats
11. The Royal Box
12. The stage pocket
13. The pitch

PLAYERS' TUNNEL

Once the players are ready, they fire themselves up and the noise of nearly 90,000 fans hits their ears as they wait in the tunnel. Here they meet their opponents for the first time and on a signal from the ref they head for the famous turf and it's game on!

As you leave Wembley, one thing's for sure, as you look back at the huge arch, it will be an experience that will stay in your mind for a long time and you'll definitely want to come back when England are in the house!

If our behind-the-scenes tour of Wembley has whetted your appetite you can find out more and book an official Wembley Stadium tour here: www.wembleystadium.com/Wembley-Tours.aspx

Wembley Stadium graphic © Gregory Gibbon/Foster + Partners

ROY HODGSON
MANAGER

Roy has taken charge of 19 teams, including four national sides, in eight different countries in his almost 40 years as a manager. So he really knows the game inside out and is one of the world's best coaches. He managed England at Euro 2012, led them to the 2014 World Cup in Brazil and so far the team have a 100% record in qualifying for Euro 2016.

PLACE OF BIRTH

Croydon
Croydon is 271km (169 miles) from St George's Park but only 21 miles (34km) from England's home, Wembley. Roy could almost shout instructions from there!

ROY'S ENGLAND RECORD

WON
22

39
GAMES

DRAWN
12

LOST
5

56.4%
WIN RATE

62
PLAYERS USED

FIRST MATCH
26/05/12 NORWAY (A) 0-1
Roy got off to a winning start in Norwegian capital, Oslo's Ullevaal Stadium, thanks to a ninth-minute strike from Manchester United's Ashley Young.

ROY'S WEMBLEY RESULTS
W D W W D W W W W L L W W W W W

"IT IS A VERY PROUD DAY FOR ME. I'M A VERY HAPPY MAN TO BE OFFERED THE CHANCE TO MANAGE MY COUNTRY"

NAGEMENT

Read all about Roy and his coaches here. The England football team is in very safe hands!

5 OF ROY'S TOP ACHIEVEMENTS:

1 Roy has won eight league titles as a manager, seven in Sweden and one in Denmark.

2 He led Switzerland to the last 16 of the 1994 World Cup in America, to Euro 96 and a FIFA ranking of third in the world!

3 He took Inter Milan to the UEFA Cup Final in 1997 and Fulham to the UEFA Europa League Final in 2010.

4 He has won two Swedish Cups and one Super Cup (Denmark).

5 In 2007 he managed Finland to their highest-ever FIFA ranking of 33rd.

ENGLAND EXPECTS:
ROY'S ROLE:

Here's just some of what he has to do – with the help of his coaches of course: pick the team; choose the system the players play; tell players when they're not in the squad; coach the players; talk to the press; encourage and direct the players during play; give the team talk; welcome new players; watch Premier League matches to see who's in form; monitor injuries… and much more. It's a massive job that Roy does brilliantly!

Teams managed (there's a few!)

2012-present England
2011-12 West Bromwich Albion
2010-11 Liverpool
2007-10 Fulham
2006-07 Finland
2004-05 Viking (Norway)
2002-04 United Arab Emirates
2001 Udinese (Italy)
2000-01 FC Copenhagen (Denmark)
1999-2000 Grasshopper (Switzerland)
1999 Inter Milan
1997-98 Blackburn Rovers
1995-97 Inter Milan (Italy)
1992-95 Switzerland
1990-92 Neuchatel Xamax (Switzerland)
1985-89 Malmo (Sweden)
1983-84 Orebro (Sweden)
1982 Oddevold (Sweden)
1982 Bristol City
1976-80 Halmstad (Sweden)

SIX THINGS YOU MIGHT NOT KNOW ABOUT ROY

- The German FA were interested in Roy when they were searching for a new manager in 1998.
- Roy speaks seven languages (yes seven!): English, French, Finnish, German, Italian, Norwegian and Swedish.
- Roy started out playing at Crystal Palace, but most of his football on the pitch was at non-league level.
- Roy was knighted by Finland for his services to their national football team in 2012.
- Roy used to work as a PE teacher. (More laps everyone!)
- Roy is England's 13th permanent manager.

RAY LEWINGTON
ASSISTANT MANAGER
England Matches as Assistant Coach: 39

Every manager needs a No.2 they can trust and Roy Hodgson already knew what a good coach Ray was from their three successful years side by side in the Fulham dugout. With bags of experience as player, coach and manager, Ray started off by helping England just for Euro 2012 but soon made the job of Assistant Coach his own. Together, they make a perfect partnership.

DID YOU KNOW? Midfielder Ray became Fulham's player-coach at the age of just 29! He kept the job for four years.

FIRST MATCH
26/05/12 NORWAY (A) 0-1

PLACE OF BIRTH

Lambeth Lambeth in south London is 238km (148 miles) from St George's Park but only 19km (12 miles) from England's home, Wembley. Just a goal kick away!

OTHER COACHES

GARY NEVILLE
COACH
With 85 caps, he's the most-capped right-back in England's history. The Manchester United legend, known for his intelligent defending, was appointed as an England coach in May 2012.

DAVID WATSON
GOALKEEPING COACH
Former England Under-21s and Barnsley goalkeeper Dave is a highly-rated goalkeeping coach. He joined the England coaching team just before Euro 2012.

COUNTER-ATTACK!

A desperate opposition manager has resorted to dirty tactics! Before a big match he has sneaked into the England dressing room and muddled up Roy's tactics board. Can you help England win the match by putting the seven mistakes right before Roy sees them and goes mad? Answers are at the bottom of the page:

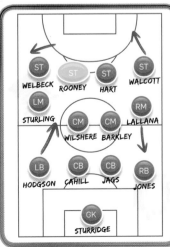

ST WELBECK, ST ROONEY, ST HART, ST WALCOTT
LM STURLING, RM LALLANA
CM WILSHERE, CM BARKLEY
LB HODGSON, CB CAHILL, CB JAGS, RB JONES
GK STURRIDGE

Answers: 13 players in a 4-4-4 line-up; Hodgson at left-back; Hart up front; Sturridge in goal; Sterling misspelt as Sturing; Rooney counter is wrong colour (yellow) and oval-shaped; penalty area has been redrawn as a semi-circle instead of a rectangle.

9

COUNTDOWN

TO A BIG ENGLAND GAME AT WEMBLEY

An England game at Wembley is a massive deal. Days before the game, the ground staff will get the pitch in A1 condition. The stadium will be cleaned and new advertising posters, banners and hoardings go up. The transport police will make sure everyone gets to and from the game safely. The stage will be set.

Up and down the land, people sit on the edge of their sofas watching the game on TV, biting their nails and then leaping up and down as England score, scattering their snacks everywhere!

But of course nothing beats actually going to Wembley to watch England live! Here we look at the preparations that have been going on for days before the referee finally blows his whistle to get the match underway.

MATCHDAY

9.00am:
There is a buzz in the air across the country. Everyone knows there is a big game on tonight. Radios crackle with big match news and TVs show interviews with Roy Hodgson and Wayne Rooney. Smartphones hum with stories of who's out injured and who's playing and in workplaces and schools everywhere, the names of England players are on everyone's lips.

10.00am:
No training for the England players today! Trains, cars, coaches and planes begin to head for London. Some fans will have already arrived the night before and some will have taken the whole day off specially. Destination for them all: Wembley Stadium!

11.00am:
The TV company screening the action checks that its cameras are all in position and working. The pitch is mowed one last time.

The last training session at St George's Park on the day before a big match!

Midday
Roy announces his team. Suddenly tonight's line-up is all over the media, with experts and fans all having their say on Roy's line-up. There's always something to talk about with England!

2.00pm:
The ground staff continue their final preparations to the pitch. Wembley is normally in superb condition, so there's nothing to worry about!

2.30pm:
The ref arrives to check the pitch is in playable condition. This isn't normally a problem at Wembley, unless the weather is really bad!

3.00pm:
The transport police get ready as the first trickle of England fans begin to head for Wembley. The players take a late, light lunch.

3.30pm:
The England team leave St George's Park by coach. They are taken to Lichfield Valley Train Station and get the train to Watford Junction, where they will board their final coach to Wembley. They'll soon be at the stadium for the big game!

4.00pm:
Arriving on Olympic Way, the smell of fried onions and hotdogs wafts through the air as afternoon slowly turns to evening and there are all sorts of stands selling England scarves, flags and badges. The tension is starting to crank up .

4.30pm:
The matchday stewards move into place as Wembley Stadium opens its gates and the first fans are in through the turnstiles. Those who haven't been there before will gasp at the size and magnificence of the stadium.

6.00pm:
The England team arrives at Wembley. The players may have had a light snack such as cereal bars or fruit to ensure they have lots of energy for the game. Normally, they arrive 75 minutes before a friendly and 90 minutes before an international qualifier. But tonight it's a vital Euro 2016 qualifier, so they're here nice and early. As the England coach draws into Wembley, fans try to catch a glimpse of their heroes.

6.30pm:
The players get stripped for action and pull on their England shirts and tracksuits. When they are ready, Roy gives his team talk, issuing final crucial tactics. Outside the atmosphere is really building as the fans pour into Wembley and the noise level rises so they can hardly hear each other as they chat about the match and take pictures of the pitch on their smartphones. Inside the England players are getting ready in the dressing room.

England mascots Paws, Mane and Roary entertain the crowd.

6.45pm:
On the pitch, the sprinklers spring into life to keep the playing surface nice and slick for England's passing game. In the referee's office, the ref briefs his team of assistants with key information regarding tonight's game.

7.00pm:
To a thrilled ripple from the crowd, the players from both teams take to the pitch to get used to the surroundings and for a light warm-up session. The fans glance up from their programmes and watch mesmerised as their favourite England players practise.

Jack Wilshere and Calum Chambers relax in the calm before the storm!

7.15pm:
The players from both teams return to their dressing rooms. England are as usual in Dressing Room 1 and their opponents in Dressing Room 2. Both managers deliver their final battle-cries and prime their players. The players are now really pumped up. Then it's out into the tunnel where the players eyeball their opposite numbers for the first time. They can hear 90,000 fans singing their hearts out in the stadium.

7.20pm:
To a mighty roar from the Wembley crowd that shakes the place to its foundations, the teams emerge from the tunnel on the halfway line.

7.30pm:
The teams line up and are introduced to the VIPS. "God Save Our Gracious Queen" rings around the stadium as England fans sing their hearts out. The anthems of both countries are of course sung.

7.45pm:
The TV cameramen train their cameras on the pitch. The ref checks the number of players on the pitch and that his assistants are ready. He signals to both goalkeepers that the game is about to begin. There is a moment of hush and then he blows his whistle. And after a long day of build-up and waiting, the crowd lets rip with a might roar. It's game on. At last!

8.30pm:
Half-time. Players take on fluid via oranges and refuelling drinks. The managers give their team talks and might shout a bit if they are losing!

9.20pm:
Final whistle. England win a brilliant game and Wayne Rooney hits his first England hat-trick! The players thank the fans for their brilliant support. Everyone goes home happy! If the fans race home, they'll catch the match highlights on telly!

ST GEORGE'S PARK
– INSPIRING POTENTIAL IN EVERYONE!

For years everyone talked about how a home was needed for English football to help us become world-beaters. On 9 October 2012 it finally arrived when St George's Park was opened by Prince William and the wraps were taken off an absolutely jaw-dropping facility. It is like a giant school of football, where coaches, managers, referees and players come to learn about the game and train. One day the hope is that we will produce an England team to conquer the world and there is no more inspiring place than St George's Park to do that. Take a tour with us now, we think you're gonna like it!

St George's Park cost £105m to build and is set in 330 acres in Staffordshire near Burton-on-Trent, slap-bang in the middle of the country, so players can reach it easily. All 24 of England's national teams stay and train there before they play. There is a 228-bed hotel, 12 outdoor pitches, a full-size indoor 3G pitch, recovery and sports science areas and a massive indoor sports hall. St George's Park isn't just world class, it's totally awesome!

DID YOU KNOW?
The Nike Academy for young players hoping to become pros is based at St George's Park.

WEMBLEY REPLICA PITCH
This pitch is simply stunning. That's because it's mainly reserved for the England senior team. It is exactly the same in every way as the pitch at Wembley Stadium, which helps the players be prepared for big games there. Like Wembley, the pitch is made from Desso Grassmaster, a type of grass which is 97% natural and 3% artificial grass which mean no divots and less wear and tear. This is also where the 'Open Training' takes place – so all those images of England training you see on TV are filmed here!

Synthetic fibres are inserted into the grass for a tougher pitch.

SIR ALF RAMSEY PITCH
The Sir Alf Ramsey Pitch is a full-size indoor 3G pitch. It is one of only a few full-size indoor artificial pitches in England; it is the biggest pitch at St George's Park and cost £1m to put in. There are 200 tons of compressed rubber under it to control the bounce and they do actually water it every now and then!

DID YOU KNOW?
St George's Park is in the heart of The National Forest and Prince William planted the eight millionth tree in the forest at St George's Park.

FUN FACT!
ST GEORGE'S PARK WAS BUILT IN JUST 15 MONTHS. AMAZING!

60M SPRINT TRACK
The 60m sprint track is part of the Michael Johnson Performance Academy. Pressure plates can be put into the track to check out a runner's style. The track runs alongside the Sir Alf Ramsey pitch.

OPEN TO EVERYONE!

You might be surprised to learn that there is a lot more to St George's Park than just football. All sorts of sports teams train there, including the England rugby team, the GB basketball team and the GB hockey team. It's not just for sports stars either. A lot of the facilities are open to everyone so you could even train or play here!

THE RUNNING HILL

The running hill is 30 metres long and has a 20° incline! That's pretty steep!

PETER SHILTON GOALKEEPING AREA

Other amazing facilities at St George's Park are the Peter Shilton Goalkeeping Area, the ultra-steep Running Hill and the ContiWarmUp Pitch. Check out our map to see more.

ENGLAND TRAIN, THEN CATCH A TRAIN!

If the England squad are meeting up for more than a day before an important match they'll usually come to St George's to train and stay. But if they're only meeting up for a day before a friendly they often meet at The Grove Hotel at Watford and train there or at London Colney, Arsenal's training ground.

BLIND FOOTBALL PITCH

The dedicated blind football pitch opened in October 2014 and the synthetic surface is perfect for this kind of football.

SITE MAP

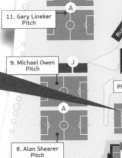

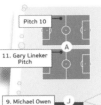

12. Gordon Banks Pitch

Pitch 10

11. Gary Lineker Pitch

9. Michael Owen Pitch

8. Alan Shearer Pitch

7. Sir Alf Ramsey Pitch

Pitch 6

Changing Rooms & Football Centre Reception

Peter Shilton Goalkeeping Area

Running Hill

Sand Pit

Pitch 14

Pitch 4

Pitch 5

Exit to Pitches

Coach Drop Off & Hotel Entrance

Hilton

Coach Parking

3. Paul Ince Pitch

2. David Beckham Pitch

Outdoor Leadership Centre

ContiWarmUp Pitch

Entrance/Exit

1. Kelly Smith Pitch

low us @FA

A Training Pitches	F GROUND FLOOR 25,000 sq ft. Learning Zone
B Elite Desso Pitch	
C Full-size Indoor 3G Pitch	G Hilton Hotel
D Football Centre	H Health Club & Spa
+ Dugout	I Conference & Banqueting
+ Perform Centre	J Pavilion
+ Sports Medicine and Sports Science	
+ Human Performance Lab	Pitch with Undersoil Heating
+ Physiotherapy and rehabilitation	Pitch with Floodlights
+ Hydrotherapy suite	
+ Medical facilities	
+ Strength and Conditioning Gym	
E Indoor Futsal Sports Hall	

THE SPORTS MEDICINE AND EXERCISE CENTRE

The Sports Medicine and Exercise Centre at St George's Park is called Perform. It includes a Strength & Conditioning zone with loads of high-tech gym equipment; a Hydrotherapy area with three pools designed to aid recovery, and a Sports Performance area where medical tests are done, which boasts an anti-gravity machine, an altitude chamber and a Batak board to test players' reactions. This is the first room that a player will come through on their journey to recovery.

All the gym equipment in the Strength & Conditioning zone faces the pitches to inspire players to recover more quickly!

In the underwater treadmill pool, cameras and jets are linked to computers that allow the physios to see exactly what's going on.

The anti-gravity machine uses NASA technology, and helps players recover from injuries.

NIKE FUTSAL SPORTS HALL

This sports hall is just huge! Three basketball courts, three tennis courts and three netball courts can fit in here all at the same time. Futsal, a kind of football played on a small pitch with a smaller ball, is played here as well as lots of other sports!

Futsal is a great way to improve your touch!

BILLY WRIGHT DRESSING ROOM

There are two elite dressing rooms at St George's Park: the Billy Wright dressing room, named after the former Wolves and England captain, and the Lyndon Lynch dressing room, named after the former Team GB Paralympic football coach. The Billy Wright elite dressing room is two-and-a-half times bigger than the Lyndon Lynch. Both dressing rooms are very similar to Wembley so players get used to them when they play there.

AUTOGRAPH WALL

One of the brilliant things at St George's Park is the Autograph Wall. It's close to the Wembley replica pitch and loads of top players and famous people have signed it.

ROY HODGSON

WAYNE ROONEY

SIR GEOFF HURST

We've picked out a few famous England stars for you. Can you spot any more?

If you would like more information about booking a tour at St George's Park, please scan this QR code

You won't be disappointed if you go!

13

GOALKEEPER

USUAL SHIRT NUMBER

HART
1

Four years earlier, Joe was in non-league football.

ENGLAND DEBUT
01/06/08 TRINIDAD & TOBAGO (A) 0-3
Joe replaced veteran David James at half-time and kept a clean sheet.

26
OF JOE'S 50 ENGLAND APPEARANCES HAVE BEEN HOME FIXTURES

From promising League 2 keeper to England's No.1 in two years: that was Joe's amazing journey. But it's not the whole story. It was while on loan at Birmingham that he really shone. Confident Joe has great presence and is such a superb shot-stopper that Lionel Messi called him a 'phenomenon'.

D.O.B. 19/04/87
Height: 1.96m
Weight: 89kg

Domestic clubs:
Manchester City (2006-present)
Birmingham City (2009-10 loan)
Blackpool (April-May 2007 loan)
Tranmere Rovers (January 2007 loan)
Shrewsbury Town (2003-06)

ENGLAND
25
CLEAN SHEETS

PLACE OF BIRTH

Shrewsbury
Shrewsbury is 92km (57 miles) from St George's Park but it's 253km (157 miles) from England's home Wembley. That's roughly 4600 goal kicks away!

JOE
HART

DID YOU KNOW?
Sports-mad Joe was head boy for his final year at his school in Shropshire.

Scan this QR code with your smart device to see some of Joe's best moments in an England shirt on the official England YouTube channel, FA TV.

FATV

WE'RE WATCHING YOU!

Almost three million fans (2,908,158) have seen Joe play for England – that's the same as the population of Lithuania, one of England's Euro 2016 rivals.

Joe has taken **344** goal kicks for England. If it takes ten seconds to spot the ball, and whack it up the field, he's spent about an hour taking England goal kicks.

50 CAPS

PRE-MATCH ROUTINE
Getting his mind in the right zone is the most important thing for Joe just before a game.

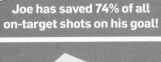

74%
TOP STOPS
Joe has saved 74% of all on-target shots on his goal!

> "I'M A SOLDIER. I'M A PLAYER. I JUST WANT TO PLAY AS MUCH AS I CAN FOR MY TEAM AND FOR MY COUNTRY."

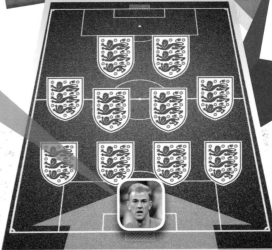

OFF THE PITCH
Joe enjoys playing golf, watching cricket and spending time with his family and friends. He was a talented cricketer as a boy!

GOALKEEPER
(Right-footed)
Joe is not only England's No.1, but one of the best goalkeepers in the world.

HEAT MAP

England's options:

Page 16   Page 18

POSITION

NICKNAME:
Joe!
His real first name is Charles!

Freak Kick!
Joe's an amazing keeper, but even he can't keep out one of these crazily twisting free kicks. Can you work out which one has beaten him?

A B C

Answer: C

8 CAPS

USUAL SHIRT NUMBER

FOSTER
13

After a two-year break from international football, the highlight of Ben's return to England action was his brilliant clean sheet v. Costa Rica in a 0-0 draw in the 2014 World Cup. With superb reflexes, the athletic West Bromwich Albion keeper is a vital part of the England goalkeeping line-up.

PLACE OF BIRTH

Leamington Spa
Leamington Spa is 87km (54 miles) from St George's Park but it's 145km (90 miles) from England's home Wembley. Ben should be one of the first to training!

Domestic clubs:

West Bromwich Albion
(2011-May 2012 loan; 2012-present)

Birmingham City
(2010-12)

Watford
(2005-07 loan)

Manchester United
(2005-10)

Wrexham
(Jan-May 2005 loan)

Kidderminster
(Oct-Nov 2004 loan)

Bristol City
(Nov-Dec 2002 loan)

Stoke City
(2002-05)

Racing Club Warwick
(2001)

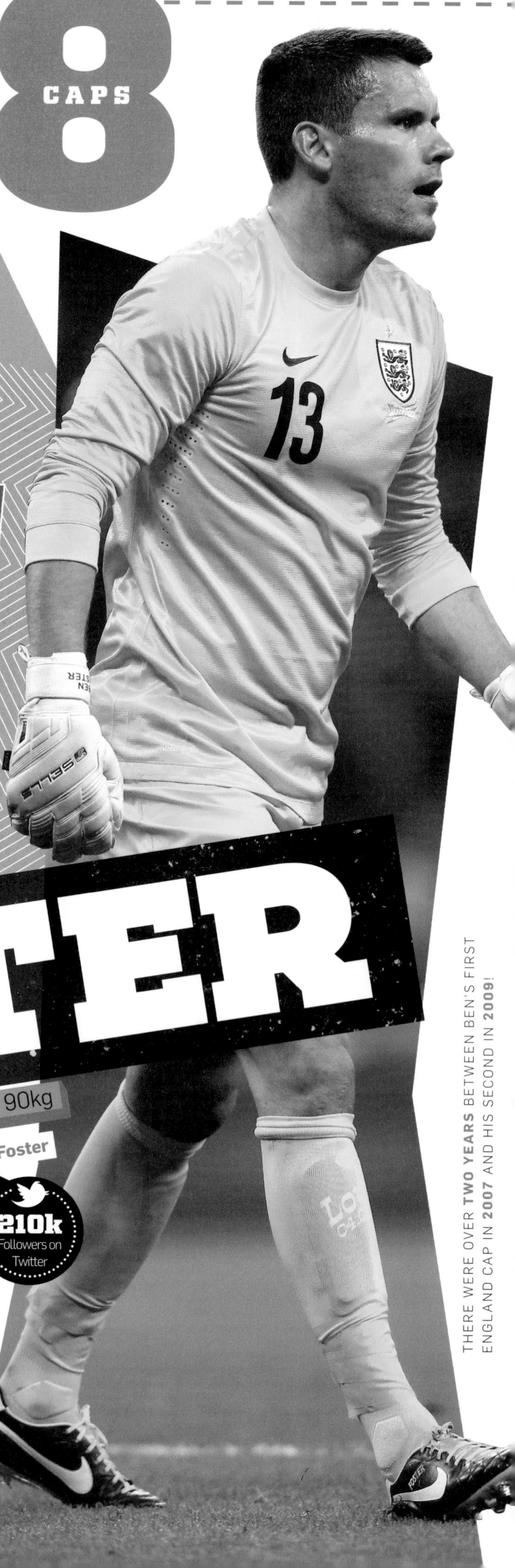

BEN FOSTER

D.O.B. 03/04/83

Height: 1.93m

Weight: 90kg

@BenFoster

210k Followers on Twitter

CLUB CLASSIC
Ben has played for four different clubs while winning his eight England caps:

➤ West Bromwich Albion 🧤🧤🧤
➤ Manchester United 🧤🧤🧤
➤ Watford 🧤
➤ Birmingham City 🧤

ENGLAND DEBUT
07/02/07 SPAIN (H) 0-1

Despite England losing this friendly, Ben had a good debut, making one great save from David Villa.

THERE WERE OVER **TWO YEARS** BETWEEN BEN'S FIRST ENGLAND CAP IN **2007** AND HIS SECOND IN **2009**!

3 CLEAN SHEETS

NICKNAME FOZZY!

LOOK! NO FEET!

BEN HASN'T HAD TO MAKE A SINGLE SAVE WITH HIS FEET IN HIS ENGLAND CAREER!

Just scan this QR code with your smart device to watch Ben and his fellow goalies, Joe Hart and Fraser Forster being put through a punishing training session here on the official England YouTube channel, FA TV.

FATV

SAFE HANDS!

Ben has by far the best record at catching the ball of any current England keeper, holding on to the ball 16 times out of the 21 saves he's made (76.2%).

76%

DID YOU KNOW?

Ben trained as a chef after leaving school and worked in a restaurant before becoming a footballer!

One of Ben's top moments was:

"PLAYING IN A WORLD CUP FOR ENGLAND AND KEEPING A CLEAN SHEET AGAINST COSTA RICA."

A LOT OF SHOTS

Ben has been England's busiest recent goalkeeper with more than one cap, facing around **3.7 shots on target per 90 minutes!**

IF THE CAP FITS

Three of these hats have something to do with Ben's professional career, but one doesn't. Which one is it?

A

B BRAZIL 2014

C

D

Answer: D

POSITION

GOALKEEPER
(Left-footed)

Ben's return to the England squad has really boosted the goalkeeping ranks.

HEAT MAP

England's options:
Page 14   Page 18

GOALKEEPER

USUAL SHIRT NUMBER

FORSTER
22

Patience pays! After seasons of being reserve goalie at Newcastle and being sent out on loan, Fraser earned rave reviews at Celtic. He improved with every game and his amazing shot-stopping, athleticism and giant presence caught Roy Hodgson's eye and led to an England debut.

D.O.B. 17/03/88
Height: 2.01m
Weight: 93kg

Domestic clubs:
Southampton
(Aug 2014-present)
Celtic
(2010-May 2012
loan; Jul 2012-14)
Norwich City
(Aug 2009-2010)
Bristol Rovers
(Aug 2009 loan)
Stockport County
(Oct-Nov 2008 loan)
Newcastle United
(2006-12)

PLACE OF BIRTH

Hexham, Northumberland
Hexham is 319km (198 miles) from St George's Park but it's 473km (294 miles) from England's home Wembley. It's almost in Scotland!

PETER CROUCH (2.03M)

2.01M

Fraser is England's tallest-ever recorded goalkeeper at 2.01m and although only the second-tallest ever England player recorded after Peter Crouch (2.03m), he is still 31cms taller than Raheem Sterling at 1.70m.

PHIL JONES (1.85M)

RAHEEM STERLING (1.70M)

FRASER FORSTER

@FraserForster

203k Followers on Twitter

BELIEVE IT OR NOT!
Coaches once saw Fraser as too small to be a keeper! "I wasn't the tallest," says Fraser, "but at 15 I started growing and didn't stop!"

ENGLAND DEBUT
15/11/13 CHILE (H) 0-2
Fraser performed well but could do nothing to stop Alexis Sanchez scoring twice in this friendly.

Scan this QR code with your smart device to hear all about Fraser Forster's goalkeeping journey on the official England YouTube channel, FA TV.

FATV

18

OFF THE PITCH

When he's not playing, laid-back Fraser likes to chill out by watching films at home, reading books and going to the cinema.

GOALKEEPER
(Right-footed)

Fraser's height and agility are huge assets for an international keeper.

HEAT MAP

England's options:

Page 14   Page 16

NICKNAME
THE GREAT WALL!

ANOTHER COUNTRY

During the 2014 World Cup, Fraser was the only England player from a non-English club (he played for Celtic before his transfer to Southampton).

HOME

DID YOU KNOW?

Fraser played more cricket and rugby than football as a boy and did not try goalkeeping until he was 13!

POSITION

19

FAST FORWARD

Fraser is the only current England goalkeeper to have played every one of his passes forwards. That's 19 out of 19 forward passes!

FRIENDLY FELLOW

Fraser hasn't played a competitive game for England yet - all three of his games have been friendlies!

FRASER'S PHRASES

Fraser is struggling to work out what the fans' flags are saying. Can you help him work it out? Answer below:

RSAREF

ETAGR

IS A

OLAGEI!

"IT'S FANTASTIC TO BE PART OF THE ENGLAND SQUAD. WE WORK REALLY HARD AND BRING THE BEST OUT OF EACH OTHER."

CAPS: 3 CLEANSHEETS: 1

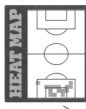

Answer: Fraser is a great goalie!

This year the FA celebrates the 50th anniversary of England hosting the 1966 World Cup. Here we show you some key England numbers since then and give you some classic all-time stats too.

1872

The world's first international featured Scotland v England in a 0-0 draw. It was nearly 100 years (1970) that the two teams played out another no-score draw!

SINCE THE 1966 WORLD CUP FINAL...

533
GAMES PLAYED

917
GOALS SCORED

259
CLEAN SHEETS

W	D	L
289	150	94

29 England's most common opponent since the 1966 World Cup final has been Scotland with **29 matches!**

14 the number of World Cups England have played in out of a possible 17!

5 England have scored five or more goals on 31 occasions since the 1966 World Cup final!

ENGL NUM

2000
ENGLAND'S 2000TH GOAL WAS SCORED BY GARETH BARRY AS ENGLAND BEAT SWEDEN 1-0 IN NOVEMBER 2011. IT WAS ALSO ENGLAND'S FIRST WIN OVER SWEDEN FOR 43 YEARS!

125 CAPS

With 125 caps, goalkeeper Peter Shilton, who played for England for twenty years (1970-1990) is the most capped England player ever!

THE DIFFERENT CONTINENTS ENGLAND HAVE PLAYED IN SINCE THE 1966 WORLD CUP FINAL.

Europe
467

Oceania **7**
Africa **8**
Asia **11**
South America **1K**

ENGLAND'S ALL-TIME LEADING GOALSCORERS

49
GOALS
SIR BOBBY CHARLTON

48
GOALS
GARY LINEKER

47
GOALS
WAYNE ROONEY

44
GOALS
JIMMY GREAVES

13-0

ENGLAND'S BIGGEST WIN WAS 13-0 OVER IRELAND IN FEBRUARY 1882!

11,704 MILES

The furthest they've travelled is Wellington, New Zealand, which is 11,704 miles away!

AND

BY

8ER5

7

7/7

England 4-0 Lithuania saw Wayne Rooney net his seventh goal in seven games.

142

There have been 142 different goalscorers, not including own goals since the 1966 World Cup final!

48,240 MINUTES

Since the start of the 2014 World Cup, England have played for a total of 48,240 minutes = 33 days and 12 hours!

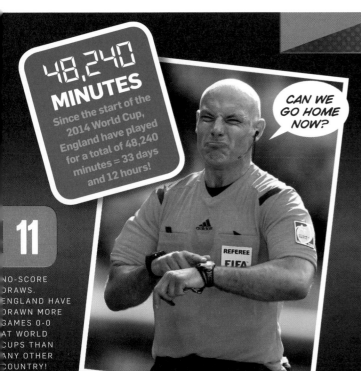

CAN WE GO HOME NOW?

11

NO-SCORE DRAWS. ENGLAND HAVE DRAWN MORE GAMES 0-0 AT WORLD CUPS THAN ANY OTHER COUNTRY!

27,571,703

27,571,703 people in total have watched England play since the 1966 World Cup final. That's more than the population of Ghana (27 million)!

5

THE NUMBER OF HAT-TRICKS GARY LINEKER SCORED FOR ENGLAND.

383

DIFFERENT PLAYERS HAVE BEEN USED.

Since the 1966 World Cup final!

DEFENDER

USUAL SHIRT NUMBER

WALKER
14

With pace to burn, attacking right-back Kyle gets the fans on the edge of their seats. The flying Spurs full-back burst onto the England scene in 2011, but was unlucky to miss out on the World Cup in 2014 due to injury. Hard-working and intelligent, Kyle's defensive game just gets better and better.

ENGLAND DEBUT
12/11/11 SPAIN (H) 1-0

Kyle replaced Scott Parker in the 85th minute as England beat the World Cup holders.

KYLE
WALKER

@kylewalker2

607k Followers on Twitter

D.O.B. 28/05/90

Height: 1.78m

Weight: 70kg

PLACE OF BIRTH

Sheffield
Sheffield is 101km (63 miles) from St George's Park but it's 253km (157 miles) from Wembley. That's 3373 lung-busting runs down the right!

GOALS, GOALS, GOALS!

England have scored **28** goals while Kyle has been on the pitch and only conceded **five!**

Domestic clubs:

Tottenham
(2009-present)

Aston Villa
(Jan-May 2011 loan)

QPR
(Sep-Dec 2010 loan)

Sheffield United
(Aug 2009-Feb 2010 loan)

Northampton
(Aug 2008-Jan 2009 loan)

Sheffield United
(2008-09)

Kyle's hero was Barcelona and Brazil full-back Dani Alves!

LIKE LIGHTNING!

Kyle is one of England's fastest players, but he knows you have to choose your runs carefully. Run smarter!

England drew 1-1 with Italy in March 2015.

WINNING RUN

W W W W W W W D W L D

Kyle has only been on the losing side for England once in 11 games, winning eight matches and drawing two.

11 CAPS

6 CLEAN SHEETS

KING OF EUROPE

All of Kyle's 11 England appearances have been against European opponents, including two full games v. San Marino.

KYLE WEARS **NIKE MAGISTA**

KYLE HAS PLAYED

900

MINUTES FOR ENGLAND

STAY ON KYLE!

PERFECT FIT!

No current England player has played more games than Kyle's 11 without being subbed. Kyle must be super-fit!

KYLE'S GOT STYLE

Three days after his England debut, Kyle helped England beat Sweden 1-0 and was named Man of the Match!

DID YOU KNOW?

KYLE WAS VOTED PFA YOUNG PLAYER OF THE YEAR IN 2012, BEATING CURRENT ENGLAND TEAM-MATES ALEX OXLADE-CHAMBERLAIN, DANIEL STURRIDGE AND DANNY WELBECK!

Scan this code to hear Kyle talking about being named Man of the Match on his full England debut on the official England YouTube channel, FA TV.

FATV

RIGHT-BACK
(Right-footed)

Kyle rockets down the right and terrorises the life out of opposing full-backs.

HEAT MAP

England's options:

 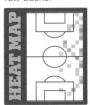

Page 24 · Page 32 · Page 34

POSITION

WALKER **RUNS!**

Normally it is Kyle who moves so fast that he's a blur. But who are these two England players racing him?

DEFENDER

USUAL SHIRT NUMBER

CLYNE
2

Confident Nathaniel forced his way into England contention after starring for Southampton. The former England Under-21 star loves to surge forward down the right wing and very few attackers get in behind him because he has the speed and awareness to get back and cover.

ENGLAND DEBUT
15/11/14 SLOVENIA (H) 3-1

On from the start Nathaniel won his first cap as Wayne Rooney collected his 100th!

CUT IT OUT!
NATHANIEL HAS INTERCEPTED PASSES MORE OFTEN THAN ANY OTHER PLAYER IN MATCHES SINCE THE START OF THE 2014 WORLD CUP: ONE EVERY 10 MINUTES 12 SECONDS!

NATHANIEL CLYNE

Weight: 67kg

Height: 1.75m

D.O.B. 05/04/91

@Nathaniel_Clyne

Stockwell, London
Stockwell in London is 235km (146 miles) from St George's Park but it's only 18km (11 miles) from Wembley. Just a hop across the capital!

PLACE OF BIRTH

82k
Followers on Twitter

Nathaniel has taken 34 throw-ins while playing for England, that's nearly nine per match!

Domestic clubs:
Southampton (2012-present)
Crystal Palace (2008-12)

4

FOUR SCORE!
England have scored in all four of Nathaniel's England appearances

WHERE'S NAT?

Usually it's just the ball that goes into the crowd, but here Nathaniel and two England team-mates are hidden among the fans. Can you spot Nathaniel and name the other two? Answers at the bottom of the page!

DID YOU KNOW? NATHANIEL JOINED CRYSTAL PALACE'S ACADEMY WHEN HE WAS ONLY EIGHT YEARS OLD!

327 TOTAL MINS PLAYED

Scan this QR code to hear Nathaniel talking about his England debut on the official England YouTube channel,

FATV

Nathaniel has **conceded four fouls on England duty.**

4 CAPS

1 CLEAN SHEET

NAT'S ALRIGHT!

Beating Scotland is always special for a proud Englishman and Nathaniel got to do it on only his second start in November 2014.

Nathaniel helped England beat Scotland 3-1!

FUN FACT!
When Nathaniel started out as a footballer, he used to play as a winger!

NATHANIEL WEARS
NIKE MAGISTA OBRA

RIGHT-BACK
(Right-footed)
Nathaniel's lightning raids down the right have always been his trademark!

HEAT MAP

England's options:

Page 22   Page 32   Page 34

POSITION

Answer: Nathaniel is the English knight on the right and his hidden team-mates are Adam Lallana and Harry Kane.

25

DEFENDER

JAGIELKA
6

PHIL JAGIELKA

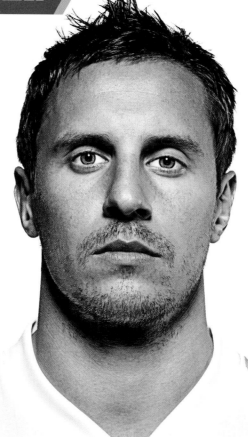

Phil is an ultra-reliable defender. The Everton captain is great in the air, determined in the tackle, reads the game brilliantly and has the pace to cover his team-mates too. He leads by example and is no slouch at the other end of the pitch either, with three England goals. Not bad for a centre-back!

D.O.B. 17/08/82

Height: 1.80m

Weight: 87kg

Domestic clubs:
Everton (2007-present)
Sheffield United (1999-2007)

PLACE OF BIRTH
Manchester
Manchester is 118km (73 miles) from St George's Park but it's a chunky 315km (196 miles) from Wembley. Wouldn't want to run it!

CENTRE-BACK
(Right-footed)
Phil's partnership with fellow centre-back Gary Cahill is growing all the time.

HEAT MAP

POSITION

OFF THE PITCH
Phil enjoys playing golf when he gets time (he's pretty good too!), has two children and loves his Shih-Tzu dog, Leo.

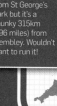

ENGLAND DEBUT
01/06/08 TRINIDAD & TOBAGO (A) 0-3
Phil made his debut in the same game as Joe Hart, coming on for Rio Ferdinand in the 46th minute.

@PJags06

155K Followers on Twitter

England's options:

Page 30   Page 32   Page 34

DID YOU KNOW?
PHIL ONCE PLAYED IN GOAL FOR SHEFFIELD UNITED AND KEPT A CLEAN SHEET!

PHIL HAS MADE

54

INTERCEPTIONS
IN ENGLAND MATCHES SINCE THE START OF THE 2014 WORLD CUP.

35 | 3
CAPS | GOALS

PHIL HAS SPENT **2272** MINUTES ON THE PITCH WITH JOE HART IN ENGLAND GAMES.

HEADS UP!

Two of Phil's three England goals have been headers!

TOP
SPEED!

Phil was named as the fastest player in the Premier League in the 2014/15 season recording a speed of 35.99kmh (22mph).

NICKNAME
JAGS!

DID YOU KNOW?

Phil's sporting hero is his older brother Stephen. Stephen was also a pro footballer and encouraged Phil to follow his dream!

Phil has both Polish and Scottish family connections, and has faced both countries twice in an England shirt.

GOALMOUTH SCRABBLE

Phil's great at organising the England defence, but can you re-organise these letters to describe one of Phil's best skills?

O L A P L K R T C T E

"YOU'VE GOT TO ENJOY THE ROLE OF BEING A DEFENDER. IF YOU ENJOY IT YOU'LL TRY HARDER AND WANT TO SUCCEED."

Scan this QR code with your smart device to hear Phil Jagielka talk about his England partnership with Gary Cahill, Leighton Baines and more on the official England YouTube channel, FA TV.

FATV

THE ROAD TO
EURO 2016

England can proudly boast a 100% record after the first five games of their Euro 2016 qualification campaign! After the disappointment of their early 2014 World Cup exit, things are looking very bright for Euro qualification so far. See you in France, we hope!

ENGLAND'S GROUP OPPONENTS

SWITZERLAND

CAPITAL: **Bern**
POPULATION: **8.1 million**
FAMOUS FOR: **FIFA and UEFA both have their headquarters there!**

ONE TO WATCH:
XHERDAN SHAQIRI

SLOVENIA

CAPITAL: **Ljubljana**
POPULATION: **2.06 million**
FAMOUS FOR: **Making their first Euro finals in 2000!**

ONE TO WATCH:
SAMIR HANDANOVIČ

LITHUANIA

CAPITAL: **Vilnius**
POPULATION: **2.94 million**
FAMOUS FOR: **Have yet to qualify for the finals of a major tournament since gaining independence.**

ONE TO WATCH:
TADAS KIJANSKAS

ESTONIA

CAPITAL: **Tallinn**
POPULATION: **1.3 million**
FAMOUS FOR: **Reaching the Euro 2012 play-off matches!**

ONE TO WATCH:
RAGNAR KLAVAN

SAN MARINO

CAPITAL: **City of San Marino**
POPULATION: **32,000**
FAMOUS FOR: **Having mainly part-time players!**

ONE TO WATCH:
ANDY SELVA

Could it be Lithuania's first major finals?

Euro 2016 will be France's third finals. As hosts, they get an automatic spot. They won in 1984 when they last hosted! But England and Harry Kane will have other ideas!

PREVIOUS
WINNERS:
 2012 SPAIN
 2008 SPAIN
 2004 GREECE
 2000 FRANCE
1996 GERMANY

DID YOU KNOW? A taller and heavier trophy was made for the 2008 tournament to reflect how big and important the competition had become!

THE FIRST FIVE GAMES

08/09/14 Switzerland 0 England 2

Referee: Cüneyt Çakır (Turkey)
Stadium: St. Jakob-Park, Basel

DID YOU KNOW?
England and Switzerland were in the same group together for the second Euro campaign in a row!

Two deadly finishes from Danny Welbeck got England up and running in Group E in an entertaining fixture in which the Swiss played their part.

09/10/14 England 5 San Marino 0

Referee: Marcin Borski (Poland)
Stadium: Wembley Stadium, London

DID YOU KNOW?
England and San Marino were in the same qualifying group for the 2014 World Cup.

Goals from Phil Jagielka, Wayne Rooney, Danny Welbeck, Andros Townsend and an own goal saw England repeat the 5-0 scoreline they had achieved against San Marino two years earlier.

12/10/14 Estonia 0 England 1

Referee: Marijo Strahonja (Croatia)
Stadium: A. Le Coq Arena, Tallinn

DID YOU KNOW?
It was Wayne Rooney's 99th England appearance but also Ragnar Klavan's 99th game for Estonia!

A brilliant Wayne Rooney free-kick saw England come through this tough test against Estonia, who played most of the second half with ten men after captain Ragnar Klavan was sent off.

15/11/14 England 3 Slovenia 1

There will be 24 teams competing in Euro 2016 for the first time; there were 16 teams in Euro 2012 hosted by Poland and Ukraine.

Referee: Olegário Benquerença (Portugal)
Stadium: Wembley Stadium, London

DID YOU KNOW?
Jordan Henderson's headed own goal was the first time England had conceded in the Euro 2016 qualifiers!

A Wayne Rooney penalty on his 100th cap and two goals from the excellent Danny Welbeck saw England bounce back from a 58th-minute Jordan Henderson own goal.

27/03/15 England 4 Lithuania 0

Referee: Pavel Královec (Czech Republic)
Stadium: Wembley Stadium, London

DID YOU KNOW?
Wayne Rooney not only scored on his 101th cap, he also hit the woodwork twice!

Goals from seasoned strikers Wayne Rooney, Danny Welbeck plus first strikes from Raheem Sterling and Harry Kane (after 79 seconds), saw England win easily.

FUN FACT:
THE OFFICIAL MASCOT FOR EURO 2016 IS CALLED SUPER VICTOR!

KEY FACTS
Tournament Name: **UEFA Euro 2016**
Number of Teams: **24**
Dates: **10/06/16-10/07/16**
Venue: **France**

EURO 2016 SCHEDULE

	BORDEAUX Stade de Bordeaux 42,000	LENS AGGLO Stade Bollaert-Delelis 35,000	LILLE MÉTROPOLE Stade Pierre Mauroy 50,100	LYON Stade de Lyon 58,000	MARSEILLE Stade Vélodrome 67,000	NICE Stade de Nice 35,000	PARIS Parc des Princes 45,000	SAINT-DENIS Stade de France 80,000	SAINT-ÉTIENNE Stade Geoffroy Guichard 41,500	TOULOUSE Stadium de Toulouse 33,000
10/06								① FRA-A2 20:00		
11/06	③ B3-B4 17:00	② A3-A4 14:00			④ B1-B2 20:00					
12/06			⑦ C1-C2 20:00			⑥ C3-C4 17:00	⑤ D3-D4 14:00			
13/06			⑩ E1-E2 20:00					⑨ E3-E4 17:00		⑧ D1-D2 14:00
14/06	⑪ F3-F4 17:00								⑫ F1-F2 20:00	
15/06			⑬ B2-B4 14:00		⑮ FRA-A3 20:00		⑭ A2-A4 17:00			
16/06		⑯ B1-B3 14:00		⑰ C2-C4 17:00				⑱ C1-C3 20:00		
17/06						㉑ D1-D3 20:00			⑳ D2-D4 17:00	⑲ E2-E4 14:00
18/06	㉒ E1-E3 14:00				㉓ F2-F4 17:00		㉔ F1-F3 20:00			
19/06			㉖ A4-FRA 20:00	㉕ A2-A3 20:00						
20/06									㉘ B4-B1 20:00	㉗ B2-B3 20:00
21/06	㉜ D4-D1 20:00	㉛ D2-D3 20:00			㉙ C2-C3 17:00		㉚ C4-C1 17:00			
22/06			㉟ E2-E3 20:00	㉞ F4-F1 17:00		㊱ E4-E1 20:00			㉝ F2-F3 17:00	
25/06		㊴ WD-3B/E/F 20:00						㊳ WB-3A/C/D 17:00	㊲ RA-RC 14:00	
26/06			㊶ WC-3A/B/F 17:00	㊵ WA-3C/D/E 14:00						㊷ WF-RE 20:00
27/06						㊹ RB-RF 20:00		㊸ WE-RD 17:00		
30/06					㊺ W37-W39 20:00					
01/07			㊻ W38-W42 20:00							
02/07	㊼ W41-W43 20:00									
03/07								㊽ W40-W44 20:00		
06/07				㊾ W45-W46 20:00						
07/07				㊿ W47-W48 20:00						
10/07								51 W49-W50 20:00		

(Group matches: 10/06–22/06; Last 16: 25/06–27/06; QF: 30/06–03/07; SF: 06/07–07/07; F: 10/07)

GROUP
A
B
C
D
E
F

W=Winner,
R = Runner-up,
3 = Third-placed

Kick-off times are CET.

UEFA will publish the final match schedule after the draw on 12 December 2015.

USUAL SHIRT NUMBER

CAHILL
5

ENGLAND DEBUT
03/09/10 BULGARIA (H) 4-0

Gary came on as a 57th-minute sub for Michael Dawson.

Tall England stopper Gary shows what you can do if you just believe in yourself and work hard. Loaned out as a young pro, he has reached the top with Chelsea and England. A terrific tackler, awesome in the air, Gary and Phil Jagielka make a great partnership. He's not bad in front of goal either!

PLACE OF BIRTH

Dronfield, North Derbyshire
Dronfield is 82km (51 miles) from St George's Park but it's 243km (151 miles) from England's home Wembley. Gary's come a long way!

Gary has travelled **33,654 MILES** while on England duty!

D.O.B. 19/12/85

Height: 1.93m

Weight: 86kg

GARY
CAHILL

@GaryJCahill

GARY ALWAYS PUTS HIS LEFT SHINPAD ON BEFORE HIS RIGHT.

DID YOU KNOW?

In June 2012, Gary unfortunately broke his jaw during a 1–0 win v. Belgium and had to miss Euro 2012.

605k
Followers on Twitter

Domestic clubs:
Chelsea
(2012-present)
Bolton Wanderers
(2008-12)
Sheffield United
(2007-08 loan)
Burnley
(2004-05 loan)
Aston Villa
(2004-08)

MILES AWAY

Gary has passed the ball further than any other England player since the start of the 2014 World Cup - a total of 5.4 miles!

Scan this QR code to hear Gary talking about his career on the official England YouTube channel, FA TV.

FATV

GARY HAS PLAYED **2954** MINUTES FOR ENGLAND

OFF THE PITCH
Gary likes to chill out by going to the cinema or playing golf.

86 MINS 53 SECS PER GAME

No current outfield player has spent longer on the pitch per game than Gary's 86 minutes 53 seconds.

CENTRE-BACK
(Right-footed)
Cool and classy in defence, Gary's dangerous when going up for set plays.

HEAT MAP

England's options:

Page 26   Page 32   Page 34

POSITION

NO WAY PAST!
Gary has helped England keep **18 CLEAN SHEETS!**

3 GOALS

BLOCKED 23

GARY HAS BLOCKED MORE SHOTS THAN ANY CURRENT ENGLAND PLAYER.

34 CAPS

NICKNAME
GAZ!

FACE TO FACE

Unusually, Gary's got himself in a muddle with another England star here. Can you work out who the other player is?

5.4 MILES!

Answer: Joe Hart

CHRIS SMALLING

@ChrisSmalling

USUAL SHIRT NUMBER

SMALLING
12

16 CAPS

Chris leapt from non-league football to full England international in just over three years, but he had already played for England schoolboys, the Under-20s and Under-21s. The Man Utd star is intelligent, athletic, strong in the air and in the tackle and can play centre-back or right-back.

D.O.B. 22/11/89

Height: 1.94m

Weight: 90kg

Domestic clubs:
Manchester United (2010-present)
Fulham (2008-10)
Maidstone United (2007-08)

PLACE OF BIRTH

Greenwich, London
Greenwich in London is 233km (145 miles) from St George's Park but it's only 30km (19 miles) from Wembley. Chris could easily nip across the capital!

BIG FOR SMALLING!
As Roy Hodgson freshened his squad, Chris made his World Cup debut v. Costa Rica in June 2014 and helped England keep a clean sheet in a 0-0 draw.

1198 TOTAL MINS PLAYED

CHRIS RATES WAYNE ROONEY AS THE BEST FINISHER HE'S PLAYED WITH!

DID YOU KNOW?
Chris and Roy Hodgson both played for Maidstone United. It was Roy who signed Chris from the non-league club for Fulham!

ENGLAND DEBUT **02/09/11 BULGARIA (A) 0-3**
Chris enjoyed a winning debut at right-back as Wayne Rooney scored twice in this Euro 2012 qualifier.

93K Followers on Twitter

JUST UNDER A MILLION PEOPLE HAVE WATCHED CHRIS PLAY FOR ENGLAND (928,309) - ROUGHLY THE SAME AS THE POPULATION OF DJIBOUTI IN AFRICA.

Chris has taken free-kicks in his England career so far! **8**

DEFENDER
(Right-footed)

Chris is a versatile defender with pace, power and intelligence in his locker!

HEAT MAP

England's options:

Page 26 | Page 30 | Page 34

POSITION

56%

Chris has won 56% of the England games he's played in.

CHRIS ALWAYS DOES HIS LEFT BOOT UP BEFORE HIS RIGHT!

"When we play internationals they'll often embroider an England logo on them so those boots are nice to keep."

CHRIS WEARS **NIKE TIEMPO**

92.9%
(118/127)

PASS RATE

Chris has completed the highest percentage of passes of any England defender in matches since the start of the 2014 World Cup.

Scan this QR code with your smart device to listen to Chris Smalling explaining why he loves working with Roy Hodgson on the official England YouTube channel, FA TV.

FATV

BOTTOM TO TOP!

Chris was only one of two England players in the 2014 World Cup squad to have played senior football at a lower level than the Football League: he played for Maidstone, while Joe Hart appeared for Shrewsbury in the Football Conference.

PITCH INVASION!

Chris doesn't make many mistakes, but can you spot six things that are in this picture that shouldn't be there?

Answer: Bucket of cleaning products, kitten, popcorn, hamburger, disco ball & balloons.

USUAL SHIRT NUMBER

JONES 15

Phil has everything you need to be a world class defender. Ferocious in the tackle, powerful in the air and above all a brilliant reader of the play, his favourite position is centre-back but he is often asked to play right-back or defensive midfield. Still only 23, he could be England captain one day.

ENGLAND DEBUT
07/10/11 MONTENEGRO (A) 2-2

It was a tough match for a debut, but 19-year-old Phil impressed at right-back in this Euro qualifier.

PLACE OF BIRTH

Preston
Preston is 151km (94 miles) from St George's Park but it's a huge 349km (217 miles) from Wembley. That's a lot more than a box-to-box run!

15 CAPS

D.O.B. 21/02/92

Height: 1.85m

Weight: 72kg

Domestic clubs:
Manchester United (2011-present)
Blackburn Rovers (2009-2011)

7 CLEAN SHEETS

Phil always tracks back. Ask Graziano Pellè!

PHIL JONES

6

SIX OF PHIL'S 15 GAMES HAVE BEEN DRAWS!

Scan this QR code with your smart device to see Phil Jones talking about England's eventful 2-2 draw with Ecuador in England's second warm-up game before the 2014 World Cup on the official England YouTube channel, FA TV.

@PhilJones4

1.88m Followers on Twitter

WHERE'S MY PASSPORT?
Phil has travelled an average of 1186 miles per match to play for England.

FATV

AT THE DOUBLE!

9 18

England have conceded nine goals while Phil's been playing but scored double that, 18!

BACK FOUR BUDDIES

Phil has spent the most time on the pitch for England with Gary Cahill - they've played together for 731 minutes.

WARNING! DANGER!

Phil has made 33 interceptions for England since the start of the World Cup 2014!

Wayne Rooney rates Phil as one of the toughest players he's ever faced!

DEFENDER/ MIDFIELDER

(Right-footed)

Phil has an enormous engine and shows total commitment wherever he plays.

HEAT MAP

England's options:

Page 26   Page 30   Page 32

STAYING IN SHAPE

To be a footballer, you've got to stay in shape. So which one of these outlines matches Phil's picture? Answers below:

A
B
C
D

Answer: C

TOP TIP: SIR ALEX FERGUSON ONCE SAID THAT PHIL COULD BECOME MAN UTD'S 'BEST EVER PLAYER'.

OFF THE PITCH

Phil enjoys golf, basketball and loves his dogs. He's interested in DJ-ing and Dubai is his favourite place to go on holiday.

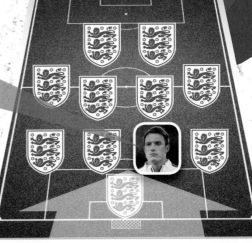

POSITION

73%

73% of Phil's appearances have been in friendlies!

Norway is the only team Phil has played twice!

35

Left Puzzle

1) I was born in?
a) Bournemouth
b) Leighton Buzzard
c) St Albans
d) Cambridge

2) My first club was?
a) Southampton
b) Northampton
c) Arsenal
d) Burnley

3) I played at?
a) U19 level for England
b) England Schoolboys
c) Only England senior level
d) U18, U19 and Under-21 level for England

4) I made my England debut against?
a) Costa Rica
b) China
c) Chile
d) Canada

5) I have?
a) Never scored for England
b) Scored one goal for England
c) Scored an own goal for England
d) Scored two goals for England

6) My grandfather is?
a) English
b) Irish
c) French
d) Spanish

SO... WHO AM I?

Now you've had a go, write your guess in this box. Or you could always use our special clue to help you!

Not guessed it yet? OK then,
HERE'S A CLUE:
My surname rhymes with banana!

Right Puzzle

1) I was born in?
a) Kendall
b) Kirkby
c) London
d) Wolverhampton

2) My first club was?
a) West Ham
b) Everton
c) Nottingham Forest
d) Wigan

3) I am?
a) 1.70m tall
b) 1.93m tall
c) 1.83m tall
d) 1.80m tall

4) I made my England debut against?
a) Ecuador
b) Spain
c) Egypt
d) Iceland

5) I have?
a) Never scored for England
b) Scored one goal for England
c) Scored an own goal for England
d) Scored four goals for England

6) I have played in?
a) No major cup finals
b) One major cup final
c) Five major cup finals
d) Two major cup finals

SO... WHO AM I?

Now you've had a go, write your guess in this box. Or you could always use our special clue to help you!

Not guessed it yet? OK then,
HERE'S A CLUE:
I'm never *late on* in England games!

36

Answer: Adam Lallana. Correct sequence: c) a) d) c) a) d)

Answer: Leighton Baines. Correct sequence: b) d) a) c) b) d)

IO ?

CAN YOU WORK OUT WHO THESE FOUR ENGLAND PLAYERS ARE AND THEIR SIX STEPS TO ENGLAND STARDOM!

By linking the correct answers to the questions in our multi-choice quiz, can you work out which four players we are describing below? Remember you may not be able to work out the answer to question 1, without looking at the others as well and putting together the pieces of the puzzle. Hint: if you get stuck, take a look back at the player profile pages – they'll definitely help you. You'll find the answers at the bottom of the page to check your detective work. Good luck!

1) I was born in?
a) 1981
b) 1985
c) 1987
d) 1983

2) My first pro club was?
a) Sunderland
b) Stoke
c) Southend
d) Spurs

3) I once trained as?
a) A chef
b) A vet
c) A teacher
d) A singer

4) I made my England debut against?
a) Slovenia
b) Spain
c) Sweden
d) Switzerland

5) I have?
a) Never scored for England
b) Scored one goal for England
c) Scored an own goal for England
d) Scored seven goals for England

6) I have been loaned out to?
a) Two clubs
b) No clubs
c) Five clubs
d) Three clubs

SO... WHO AM I?

Now you've had a go, write your guess in this box. Or you could always use our special clue to help you!

Not guessed it yet? OK then,
HERE'S A CLUE:
I'm great with my hands!

1) I was born in?
a) Berlin
b) Bolton
c) Bognor Regis
d) Birmingham

2) My first club was?
a) Chelsea
b) Man Utd
c) Man City
d) Aston Villa

3) My uncle was?
a) A footballer
b) A cricketer
c) An Olympic swimmer
d) A darts player

4) I made my England debut against?
a) Turkey
b) Norway
c) Sweden
d) Tunisia

5) I have?
a) Never scored for England
b) Scored five goals for England
c) Scored an own goal for England
d) Scored three goals for England

6) I like to celebrate by?
a) Singing
b) Running into the crowd
c) Knee slide
d) Dancing

SO... WHO AM I?

Now you've had a go, write your guess in this box. Or you could always use our special clue to help you!

Not guessed it yet? OK then,
HERE'S A CLUE:
I just love busting some moves after I've scored!

Answer: Ben Foster Correct sequence: d) b) a) c)

Answer: Daniel Sturridge Correct sequence: d) c) a) c) b) d)

37

DEFENDER

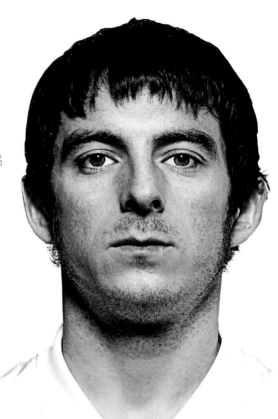

USUAL SHIRT NUMBER

BAINES
3

Hard-working Leighton is right up there with the world's best attacking left-backs. Quick and clever, he loves to raid down the left and deliver pinpoint crosses for the England forwards to gobble up. Once a left-winger, he can deliver a wicked free-kick and is deadly from the penalty spot too.

LEIGHTON LIKES TO STAND AT THE TOP OF THE D AT THE EDGE OF THE PENALTY AREA BEFORE KICK-OFF AND RE-TIE HIS LACES!

LEIGHTON
BAINES

D.O.B. 11/12/84

Height: 1.70m

Weight: 70kg

Leighton has won 19 of his England games.

13

Leighton has helped England to 13 clean sheets and the team has scored 59 goals while he's been playing!

PLACE OF BIRTH

Kirkby, Liverpool
Kirkby, Liverpool is 138km (86 miles) from St George's Park but it's 336km (209 miles) to Wembley. Don't be late, Leighton!

"**STAY FOCUSED** ON WHAT YOU WANT TO DO AND ... IF YOU'RE LUCKY AND GET TO MAKE IT AS A PROFESSIONAL FOOTBALLER THEN IT'S ALL WORTH IT."

DID YOU KNOW?

Leighton was inspired to become a footballer by his granddad who took him to Sunday League games as a boy.

ENGLAND DEBUT
03/03/10 EGYPT (H) 3-1

Leighton turned in a promising display and helped England to victory in this friendly after Egypt scored first.

64

WHEN I'M 64!

Leighton has taken 64 corners in his England career so far, more than any player in the current England squad!

FOAMING
AT THE GOALMOUTH!

The ref has gone a bit crazy with his free-kick shaving foam here. He's definitely crossed the line! Can you spot the four players hiding in the foam?

Scan this QR code with your smart device to watch Luke Shaw's superb free-kick technique on the official England YouTube channel, FA TV.

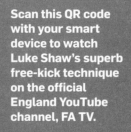

FA TV

SHAW TO SHORE

Luke has travelled the furthest on average for each of his England appearances:

2625 MILES!

Chris Smalling has played every single minute that Luke has for England – 281 minutes in total!

DID YOU KNOW?
Aged 18 and 347 days, Luke was the youngest player to appear at the World Cup 2014. He is also the second-youngest England player to play at any World Cup after Michael Owen.

6

Luke has been fouled six times on England duty.

LUKE WAS INSPIRED TO BE A FOOTBALLER BY ENGLAND GREAT, ASHLEY COLE!

"IT WAS UNBELIEVABLE TO PLAY IN A WORLD CUP GAME. THE BIGGEST STAGE IN FOOTBALL. IT IS SOMETHING I WILL LEARN FROM."

LEFT-BACK
(Left-footed)

Luke's future is so bright that he will never be *left back* in the changing room!

HEAT MAP

POSITION

England's options:

Page 38   Page 76   Page 76

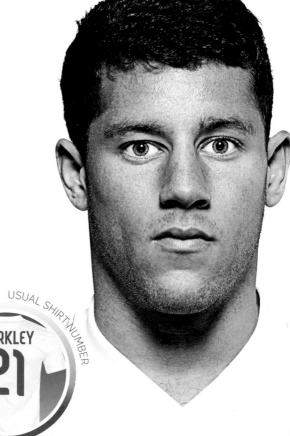

ROSS BARKLEY

Ross is a powerful midfielder who is great with both feet and has awesome close control. The sight of him in full flight has defenders panicking and puts fans on the edge of their seats. He lights up games with moments of pure brilliance and the sky's the limit for the young Everton maestro.

D.O.B. 05/12/93

Height: 1.89m

Weight: 76kg

USUAL SHIRT NUMBER

BARKLEY
21

PLACE OF BIRTH
Liverpool
Liverpool is 137km (85 miles) from St George's Park but it's a whopping 335km (208 miles) from Wembley. Better get a shift on, Ross!

12 CAPS

POSITION

MIDFIELDER
(Right-footed)
Ross has the creativity, energy and skill to unlock the meanest defences.

HEAT MAP

England's options:

Page 48 | Page 50 | Page 54

ROSS HAS REPRESENTED ENGLAND AT

UNDER-16	✓
UNDER-17	✓
UNDER-19	✓
UNDER-20	✓
UNDER-21	✓
FULL INTERNATIONAL	✓

@RBarkley20

ENGLAND DEBUT
06/09/13 MOLDOVA (H) 4-0

Ross came on in the 60th minute for Jack Wilshere and very nearly scored in this World Cup qualifier.

448 TOTAL MINS PLAYED

690,992 FANS HAVE SEEN HIM PLAY FOR HIS COUNTRY.

327k Followers on Twitter

6-6
SCORE DRAW!

Ross has faced six teams from Europe and six teams from outside Europe so far!

ONLY LUKE SHAW HAS TRAVELLED FURTHER ON AVERAGE FOR EACH OF HIS ENGLAND APPEARANCES THAN ROSS'S 2213 MILES.

NICKNAME
ROSSI!

Domestic clubs:
Everton
(2010-present)
Leeds United
(2013 Jan-Feb loan)
Sheffield Wednesday
(2012 Sep-Nov loan)

1 ASSIST

OFF THE PITCH
Ross enjoys watching films, playing video games (especially Call of Duty) and loves a good roast dinner!

All of Ross's five shots for England have been right-footed.

Scan this QR code with your smart device to watch Ross score with a wicked long-rage strike while training for England on the official England YouTube channel, FA TV.

FATV

Italy are the only team Ross has played against twice but for just 73 minutes combined.

"I DON'T FEEL PRESSURE. I BELIEVE IN MYSELF AND I KNOW WHAT I CAN DO."

DID YOU KNOW?
Ross was such a good player as an eight-year-old that he used to play for his local Under-11 side and then turn out for the Under-10s too!

BANK ON BARKLEY

Ross sets out on three of his mind-blowing dribbles. The trouble is only one of them has resulted in an England goal this time. Can you spot which one it is?

GOAL!!

A
B
C

ROSS WEARS
← NIKE HYPERVENOM

Answer: B

43

GAME

THE BIG ENGLAND CROSSWORD

What England women's international Lucy Bronze is doing here will help you answer **3 across!**

This familiar face saluting the crowd is a hint for **4 across!**

This celebrating striker will help you answer **13 down!**

What's the England team's favourite drink?

Penaltea!

These guys help the team and they can help you answer **15 across** too!

ACROSS

3. Getting the ball back into play with your hands
4. The England manager
10. If you don't score one of these, you'll never win
11. The man in the middle
12. They come in every colour these days!
14. Where you kick off
15. England need these cheering them on
16. You play on this!
18. What every team needs
19. One day we might win this again!
20. Barcelona love doing this!
21. Jags is fast!

DOWN

1. He shoots, he scores!
2. England's number one
5. Using your head
6. Where England train
7. The length of a game
8. Where England play their home internationals
9. You've got to be brave to take one of these
10. One of the England coaches
13. The England captain
17. The name of the game

TRUE OR FALSE?

1. Roy Hodgson is a former England international?

2. James Milner was once a ball boy at Leeds Utd?

3. The three lions on the England shirt come from a Royal coat of arms?

4. Wayne Rooney is the oldest ever England player to win 100 caps?

WHO GOES THERE?

Can you work out who we've cut out of this picture in this international friendly against Italy in March 2015?

CLUE: IT WAS QUITE A GOOD SHOT!

PLAYING AROUND!

Can you unscramble the names of these England players to find out who they are?

GALA RICHLY
BARKS SORELY
WATCH TOOTLE

ODD ONE OUT

Can you tell us which of these seven players is the odd one out?

WORD CHASE

Add the letters that complete the words on either side of the puzzle to create a new word to do with the England football team. We've done the first one to help you.

S	T	ERLING
		ART
LAMBE		T
ROON		Y
WELB		CK
BARK		EY
STURR		DGE
ST		NES
TOW		SEND
HENDER		ON

Why did Roy Hodgson bring pencils to Wembley?
He was hoping for a draw!

SPOT THE DIFFERENCE

Harry Kane rises the highest in this aerial battle against Italy, but can you rise to the challenge of spotting six differences between the original picture on the left and the one on the right?

CAN YOU COMPLETE THIS HEADLINE?

WA_N__OON
WI__ 100TH
AND S_ORE
ENALT!

Why did the Wembley pitch end up as a triangle?
Someone took a corner!

PRETTY AS A PICTURE!

Can you work out the names of two England players from our picture clues above? You'll need to use your imagination!

ANSWERS: The Big England Crossword: Across 3 Throw-in, 4 Roy Hodgson, 10 Goal, 11 Referee, 12 Boots, 14 Centre spot, 15 Fans, 16 Pitch, 18 Teamwork, 19 World Cup 20 Passing 21 Phil Jagielka Down: 1 striker, 2 ole Hart, 5 Header, 6 St George's Park, 7 Ninety minutes, 8 Wembley Stadium, 9 Penalty, 10 Gary Neville, 13 Wayne Rooney, 17 Football. **Who Goes There:** Andros Townsend. **Playing Around:** Gary Cahill, Ross Barkley and Theo Walcott. **Odd One Out:** Phil Jagielka is the only one who doesn't play for either Liverpool or Man Utd. **True or False?** 1. False 2. True 3. True 4. False – he's the youngest! **Can You Complete This Headline?** Wayne Rooney Wins 100th Cap and Scores Penalty! **Pretty as a Picture:** Jack Wilshere and Theo 'Three-o' Watcott! **Spot The Difference:** Dog on pitch, Gianluigi Buffon wearing green sock, Darmian's shirt name has vanished, ball is missing, Giorgio Chiellini's arm is missing and England flag added to crowd. **Word Chase:** Three Lions

45

MIDFIELDER

STERLING
11

With his pace and fearless dribbling, Raheem is a real breath of fresh air. Brave on the ball, he drives defenders nuts with his awesome trickery and is just what England need to unlock tight defences. The Liverpool star has already shown what he can do at a World Cup and the only way is up!

Domestic clubs:
Liverpool (2010-present)
QPR (2009-10)

D.O.B. 08/12/94

Height: 1.70m

Weight: 69kg

GOAL **1**

PLACE OF BIRTH

Kingston, Jamaica
Kingston, Jamaica is 7428km (4616 miles) from St George's Park but it's 7520km (4673 miles) from Wembley! Raheem is miles better!

Although he was born in Jamaica, Raheem can play for our national team because he emigrated to England when he was just five years old.

RAHEEM STERLING

@sterling31

1.23m
Followers on Twitter

Raheem celebrates tapping home his first England goal during the Euro qualifier against Lithuania.

ENGLAND DEBUT
14/11/12 SWEDEN (A) 4-2

DID YOU KNOW?

Raheem saw the new Wembley being built because his school was so close. He used to ride around outside the stadium on his BMX!

RAHEEM RUNS 'EM RAGGED!

Raheem was rated England's star player by the BBC in their 2-1 defeat to Italy at the 2014 World Cup. He was a constant threat and helped set up England's equalising goal.

OFFSIDE!

Raheem has been caught offside twice for England.

2

Raheem was one of six debutants in a match that saw Zlatan Ibrahimovic score four goals including that outrageous overhead kick!

FOUL PLAY!

Raheem gets fouled more often than any current England player – roughly 2.5 times per 90 minutes.

Scan this QR code with your smart device to watch Raheem Sterling's first England goal in the 4-0 win over Lithuania in March 2015 on the official England YouTube channel, FA TV.

FATV

MIDFIELDER
(Right-footed)

Raheem dazzles, darts and dances down the wing like only he knows how.

HEAT MAP

England's options:

Page 50 Page 58 Page 62

Raheem has Wembley tube station and stadium tattooed on his arm. They remind him of "the dream that's becoming a reality".

POSITION

3
RAHEEM HAS SET UP THREE GOALS IN HIS ENGLAND CAREER.

SHARP SHOOTER

Raheem has hit the target with an excellent 50% of his 14 shots for England.

RAZ!

NICKNAME

THE BIG MATCH!

Raheem is running the defence ragged again, but he's sent his picture into pieces too. Can you match the pieces to the empty slots to compete the picture?

① =

② =

③ =

④ =

Answer: 1. goes with d); 2. goes with a) 3. goes with b); 4 goes with c)

RAHEEM WEARS
NIKE MERCURIAL VAPOR X

USUAL SHIRT NUMBER

WILSHERE
7

1,590,207 FANS HAVE WITNESSED JACK IN ENGLAND ACTION.

JACK WILSHERE

Jack can burst past players with the ball at his feet, pick a pinpoint pass with just a wave of his wand of a left foot and do battle with the best in the midfield cauldron. He can play as defensive midfielder, but it is his vision and creativity going forward which make him so exciting.

PLACE OF BIRTH

Stevenage
Stevenage is 180km (112 miles) from St George's Park but it's only 47km (29 miles) from Wembley! Jack's bang on track!"

D.O.B. 01/01/92

Height: 1.73m

Weight: 68kg

Domestic clubs:
Arsenal
(2008-present)
Bolton Wanderers
(Jan-Jun 2010 loan)

DID YOU KNOW?

When asked to pick his favourite England player in 2014, Spain and Barcelona star Xavi said: "I think Jack Wilshere is an amazing player. Very good."

ENGLAND DEBUT
11/08/10 HUNGARY (H) 2-1

Two goals from Steven Gerrard helped England come back from 1-0 down. Jack replaced the England skipper after 83 minutes.

JACK WEARS
NIKE MAGISTA OPUS

JACK BLITZES BRAZIL!

When England beat Brazil 2-1 at Wembley in February 2013, Jack produced a brilliant performance that helped him win the game for England and the Man of the Match award.

@JackWilshere

1.81M Followers on Twitter

26
CAPS

MIDFIELDER
(Left-footed)

Jack's composure on the ball and awareness make him a dream midfielder.

HEAT MAP

England's options:

Page 42 Page 50 Page 62

OFF THE PITCH

Jack has two young children, loves spaghetti bolognese and enjoys playing FIFA - he was even on the cover of the FIFA 12 game with Wayne Rooney!

THE TATTOOS ON JACK'S ARMS ARE MAINLY TO DO WITH HIS FAMILY!

POSITION

13
EFFORTS ON GOAL FOR ENGLAND

1
WITH HEAD

8
WITH LEFT FOOT

4
WITH RIGHT FOOT

> "YOU'VE GOT THOSE THREE LIONS ON YOUR SHIRT AND YOU'VE GOT TO FIGHT AND WORK HARD FOR EACH OTHER."

PASS RATE

84%

Jack has an 84% pass completion rate since the start of the 2014 World Cup.

Scan this QR code with your smart device to watch Jack Wilshere's starring role as England beat Brazil 2-1 in February 2013 on the official England YouTube channel, FA TV.

FATV

ASSISTS: 3

JACK MADE HIS FIRST APPEARANCE IN AN ENGLAND SHIRT **BEFORE** HE HAD COMPLETED A FULL PREMIER LEAGUE GAME FOR ARSENAL.

YOUNG GUNS!

When Jack debuted for England he was the tenth-youngest ever England player, but can you put these players in age order with the youngest first? No cheating now!

A
B
C
D

Answer: Ans: a) Luke Shaw (12/07/1995); b) Raheem Sterling (08/12/1994); c) Ross Barkley (05/12/1993); d) Jack Wilshere (01/01/1992).

ADAM LALLANA

ADAM'S GRANDFATHER IS SPANISH WHICH EXPLAINS HIS UNUSUAL SURNAME!

Goalscorer and goalmaker; quick and tricky on the ball and good with either foot, it's no wonder Adam has been compared with Spanish great Andrés Iniesta. From lighting up League One with Southampton to England international, Adam's has been a long journey, but it's been so worth the wait!

USUAL SHIRT NUMBER

LALLANA
20

ENGLAND DEBUT
15/11/13 CHILE (H) 0-2

Adam looked lively for 77 minutes and was unlucky not to mark his debut with a goal before being replaced by Ross Barkley.

Domestic clubs:
Liverpool (2014-present)
Bournemouth (2007 Oct-Nov loan)
Southampton (2006-14)

D.O.B. 10/05/88

Height: 1.73m

Weight: 73kg

PLACE OF BIRTH
St Albans
St Albans is 180km (112 miles) from St George's Park but it's only 34km (21 miles) from Wembley! Let's get going! It won't take long!

734
TOTAL MINS PLAYED

OFF THE PITCH

Adam spends a lot of time with his young son Arthur, enjoys the occasional burger as a treat and used to play cricket at county level

LEFT IS ALRIGHT
Adam is good with both feet, but seven of Adam's nine shots on goal for England have been with his left foot.

LEFT 7   RIGHT 2

17
12

Adam has given away 17 fouls, but he has also been fouled 12 times in his England career.

ADAM'S FOOTBALL BOOTS WERE EMBROIDERED WITH THE ENGLAND FLAG AND 'CAP NO.1' FOR HIS ENGLAND DEBUT!

2 ASSISTS

Scan this QR code with your smart device to watch highlights of England's 1-0 World Cup warm-up win over Denmark and see Adam's assist in March 2014 on the official England YouTube channel, FA TV.

FATV

13 CAPS

ADAM HAS TAKEN 18 CORNERS FOR ENGLAND.

18

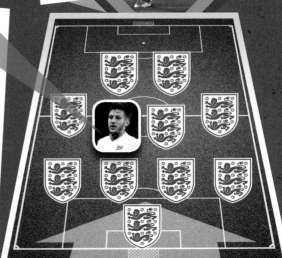

Lallana's let loose against Uruguay at the 2014 World Cup.

DID YOU KNOW?

Adam is really two-footed. He says: "I've worked with both feet since I was a kid. It's great not having to think about what foot you want to use."

MIDFIELDER
(Right-footed)

Adam adds flair, grace and drive to the England engine room!

HEAT MAP

England's options:

Page 54   Page 56   Page 58

POSITION

MIDFIELD MUDDLE!

Adam's so versatile that he shares lots of skills with his team-mates, but not normally like this! Can you spot whose head, chests and legs we've added to Adam in these two pictures?

"I'LL ALWAYS GIVE IT MY ALL AND WORK MY HARDEST."

ADAM'S ACE!

Adam came off the bench in the 59th minute to cross for Daniel Sturridge to head the only goal as England beat Denmark 1-0 in March 2014 in a friendly at Wembley.

Answers: Image 1: Jordan Henderson's torso and Andros Townsend's legs. Image 2: James Milner's head and Joe Hart's legs

51

GETTING TECHIE

Football is a simple game, but these days as teams try to find that extra edge that makes the difference between winning and losing, between the manager getting cheered off or booed off, it's all gone hi-tech crazy out there! So let's take a look at some of the exciting new technologies that are being used by England and the other top teams of the modern game. One thing's for sure, just like the players, technology's never going to stand still.

ENGLAND SHIRTS

England's 2014 World Cup shirts featured enhanced cooling technology to cope with the temperatures in Brazil. Nike's Ultra-soft Dri-FIT fabric pulls moisture away from the skin to the outside of the shirt, where it can evaporate easily. There are also mesh zones and laser cut holes for better airflow.

DID YOU KNOW?

England's 2014 World Cup white and red kits were made from recycled plastic bottles with 100% recycled polyester in the shorts, 96% recycled polyester in the shirt and 78% in the socks.

BALLS

Ball technology has moved on a long way since the early days of heavy leather balls, which could be a bit like heading a lump of concrete! These days, ball manufacturers have spent lots of money to improve the way the ball moves in the air. Nike are the official supplier of the balls used in England games, except in the World Cup finals. Nike's Ordem ball aims to give a great first touch and quick control. There are even new smart balls with built-in sensors that connect to a smartphone app via Bluetooth!

BOOTS

Anyone wearing plain old black leather boots these days looks like a bit of a dinosaur! These days boots come in every colour of the rainbow and sometimes all of them on one boot! The stud patterns and material used are changing all the time too – leather has been substituted for new form synthetic materials which make boots as light as possible. A good example of new material technology is Nike's flexible NikeSkin material which hugs your natural foot shape. There are also boots that contain a sensor and link to a smartphone app to track everything about your play from distance covered over the 90 minutes to your top speed.

Imagine Raheem Sterling wearing these 1936 boots!

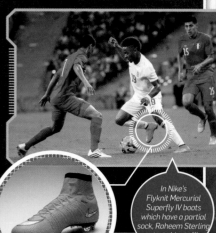

In Nike's Flyknit Mercurial Superfly IV boots which have a partial sock, Raheem Sterling struts his stuff!

A nice close-up of the Ordem ball as Wayne Rooney hits the back of the net after blasting a penalty past Slovenian goalkeeper Samir Handanovic.

GPS VESTS

England use GPS (Global Positioning System) systems in training to collect stats on speed, distance, heart rate, accelerations and decelerations. They used these vests before the 2014 World Cup.

GLOVES

Goalies' gloves have come on massively since they first appeared in the game.
There are now all sorts of gloves to suit different conditions and goalies' needs. There are good all-round gloves. Gloves with superb grip, more finger protection, gloves with pre-curved fingers, gloves with a wraparound tunnel wristband to secure the hand within the glove and warmer gloves for winter... the list is endless!

Check out these old school gloves worn by England goalkeepers Phil Parkes (left) and Peter Shilton (right) and Gordon Banks (centre) back in 1972.

GOAL-LINE TECHNOLOGY

England's recently-retired midfielder Frank Lampard's thunderous shot which hit the crossbar and crossed the line but wasn't given as a goal when England were playing Germany in the 2010 World Cup, played a huge part in FIFA deciding to bring in goal-line technology. Welcoming the technology, Frank said: "It's a no-brainer. It's been a long time coming but they got here in the end. It's a simple thing that will bring an excitement factor when it's used."

Goal-line technology was tested at Wembley Stadium for England's 1-0 victory against Belgium in June 2012 and The FA installed it for real at Wembley Stadium in time for the 2013 Community Shield.

DID YOU KNOW?

Goal-line technology was invented by Dr Paul Hawkins of British company Hawk-Eye, which also provide technology for tennis, cricket and snooker.

HOW IT WORKS!

Goal-line technology has been described as the biggest change in football for 150 years. Not to mention that it's great fun waiting to see if a goal has actually been scored! So how does it work?

1 Seven cameras located around each goal track the ball inside the goal area.

2 A computer analyses data from the cameras and, as soon as it detects that the ball has crossed the goal-line, it sends a signal to the ref's watch in a second.

3 Hawk-Eye also sends replays to TV outlets.

FOAMY FUN IS NUMBER ONE!

Goal-line technology was not the only shiny new toy on show at the 2014 World Cup, we mustn't forget the referees' new magic spray! This vanishing foamy stuff was one of the real stars of the tournament! Now players could no longer sneak forward because the foam marked the correct distance the wall should stand from the ball.

DID YOU KNOW?

The free-kick foam is the invention of Argentine journalist Pablo Silva who developed the spray called '9:15 Fairplay' – 9.15 being the distance in metres that a wall should stand from the free-kick.

THE SCIENCE

The foam is a mixture of butane, isobutane and propane gas; a foaming agent, water and other chemicals. When it leaves the can, the gas depressurises and expands, creating water-covered droplets on the field. The butane mixture later evaporates, leaving only water behind. Everybody got that? Good.

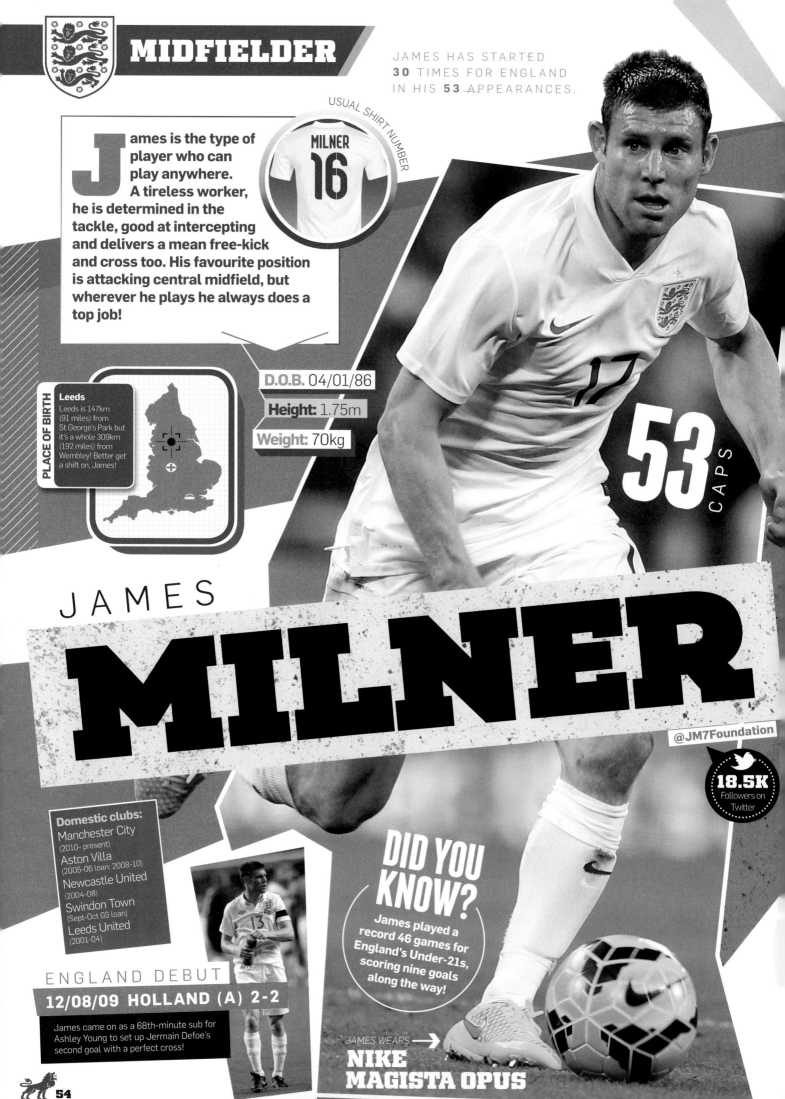

MIDFIELDER

JAMES HAS STARTED **30** TIMES FOR ENGLAND IN HIS **53** APPEARANCES.

James is the type of player who can play anywhere. A tireless worker, he is determined in the tackle, good at intercepting and delivers a mean free-kick and cross too. His favourite position is attacking central midfield, but wherever he plays he always does a top job!

USUAL SHIRT NUMBER

MILNER
16

PLACE OF BIRTH

Leeds
Leeds is 147km (91 miles) from St George's Park but it's a whole 309km (192 miles) from Wembley! Better get a shift on, James!

D.O.B. 04/01/86

Height: 1.75m

Weight: 70kg

53 CAPS

JAMES MILNER

@JM7Foundation

18.5K Followers on Twitter

Domestic clubs:
Manchester City (2010- present)
Aston Villa (2005-06 loan: 2008-10)
Newcastle United (2004-08)
Swindon Town (Sept-Oct 03 loan)
Leeds United (2001-04)

DID YOU KNOW?

James played a record 46 games for England's Under-21s, scoring nine goals along the way!

ENGLAND DEBUT

12/08/09 HOLLAND (A) 2-2

James came on as a 68th-minute sub for Ashley Young to set up Jermain Defoe's second goal with a perfect cross!

JAMES WEARS →
NIKE MAGISTA OPUS

MIDFIELDER
(Right-footed)
Versatile James can play in central midfield or on the wing on either side!

HEAT MAP

England's options:

Page 46   Page 50   Page 56

POSITION

OFF THE PITCH
James enjoys unwinding from football by walking his two dogs, playing golf and gaming on his PlayStation.

UKRAINE AGAIN!
James has played against Ukraine more than any other side: four times, making a total of 310 minutes.

GOAL
James scored his first England goal with a drilled, low shot from the edge of the area as England ran out 5-0 winners away to Moldova in a World Cup qualifier in September 2012.

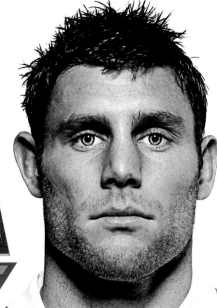

Scan this QR code with your smart device to listen to James talking about his pride in winning 50 caps for England in a 0-2 win over Switzerland in September 2014 on the official England YouTube channel, FA TV.

FATV

"IT'S A GREAT HONOUR TO REPRESENT YOUR COUNTRY AT ANY LEVEL, BUT I NEVER THOUGHT ABOUT LANDMARKS, OR 50 CAPS SO I AM VERY PROUD OF IT."

JAMES HAS TAKEN
60
CORNERS ON ENGLAND DUTY!

JAMES' GAME!

James can fit in anywhere on the pitch, but are you clever enough to puzzle out the eight words in this wordsearch?
Clue: they're all to do with James!

```
D E T E R M I N E D N E D
A S U T H G N L S Y O T P
T N H G I H T T O K X C T
P M I D F I E L D E R T A
A T N S S O R M T O S F K
S B Y T Q H N Q S T Y A E
S K L O T L A S B T L S P
T I F A V D T D V L X I T
M C R O S E I T A O O N M
R Y T S N M O M R L E C T
C M I L B T N G T P A J K
T V F C T T A C K L E A T
O D S G M I L N E R I S Y
```

MIDFIELDER

JORDAN HENDERSON

USUAL SHIRT NUMBER

HENDERSON
4

If you want a box-to-box midfielder with technical skills to match his sky-high energy levels, Jordan is your man. Everyone knows what a superb athlete he is, but since joining Liverpool, he has been developing the creative side of his game and can deliver a killer through ball with the best of them.

PLACE OF BIRTH

Sunderland
Sunderland is 278km (173 miles) from St George's Park but it's a whole 440km (273 miles) from Wembley! Just as well Jordan's got a great engine!

D.O.B. 17/06/90

Height: 1.82m

Weight: 67kg

OFF THE PITCH

Jordan relaxes by playing video games and spending time with his young daughters. Oh and he likes poached egg on toast for breakfast!

20 CAPS

ASSIST 1

JORDAN WEARS **NIKE MAGISTA OPUS**

@JHenderson

173K Followers on Twitter

ENGLAND DEBUT 17/11/10 FRANCE (H) 1-2

On from the start, it was a tough start for Jordan as England were outplayed by France and Jordan picked up a yellow card.

MIDFIELDER
(Right-footed)

Jordan has everything the modern midfielder needs to compete at the top.

HEAT MAP

Domestic clubs:
Liverpool
(2011- present)
Coventry City
(Jan-Jun 2009 loan)
Sunderland
(2008-11)

Scan this QR code with your smart device to listen to Jordan talking about his first call-up to the England squad in November 2010 on the official England YouTube channel, FA TV.

FATV

75%

75% of his England matches have been against European teams.

England's options:

Page 46   Page 50   Page 54

POSITION

"MAKE SURE YOU WORK AS HARD AS YOU CAN AND PLAY WITH A SMILE ON YOUR FACE!"

UP FOR THE CUP!
Jordan made his World Cup debut in June 2014. He played 73 minutes of the game against Italy and although England lost 2-1, Jordan's energy in the heat was vital.

THE RIGHT STUFF
Ten of Jordan's 11 shots for England have been with his right foot, but only six of his shots have been on target!

Henderson 4m

Jordan has passed the ball further than any other midfielder since the start of the 2014 World Cup: a total distance of four miles!

ENGLAND GAMES STARTED

13   20

SIDE SHOW!
It's normally easy to spot famous players, but can you work out who these famous faces are just from these side views?

A   **B**   **C**   **D**

DID YOU KNOW?
Former Under-21s captain Jordan was voted England Under-21s Player of the Year in 2013, the first year of the award.

Answers: A Raheem Sterling, B Harry Kane, C Jordan Henderson, D Fraser Forster.

USUAL SHIRT NUMBER

WALCOTT
7

ENGLAND HAVE **SCORED THREE OR MORE GOALS** IN NEARLY HALF (47.4%) OF THEO'S GAMES.

Pace, movement, intelligence and a superb attitude make Theo one of England's most feared attacking players. Famous for being picked for the 2006 World Cup before he had even made his Premier League debut, Theo is now known for his awesome wing play for both Arsenal and England. Theee-o!

THEO WALCOTT

PLACE OF BIRTH

Stanmore, Middlesex
Stanmore is 198km (123 miles) from St George's Park but it's only 9km (5.6 miles) from Wembley! It's almost in Theo's back garden!

D.O.B. 16/03/89

Height: 1.76m

Weight: 68kg

Domestic clubs:
Arsenal
(2006-present)
Southampton
(2005-06)

LATE STARTER
Theo didn't start playing football until he was ten but then scored
100 GOALS
for AFC Newbury!

MIDFIELDER
(Right-footed)
Flying down the wing, Theo is as fast as lightning and thinks as quickly too.

HEAT MAP

POSITION

England's options:

Page 46 | Page 50 | Page 56

ENGLAND DEBUT
30/05/06 HUNGARY (H) 3-1

Theo made history as England's youngest-ever player when he came on after 65 minutes replacing Michael Owen.

851K
Followers on Twitter

@theowalcott

DID YOU KNOW?
Theo played his first game for England on 30 May 2006, but didn't make his Premier League debut for Arsenal until 19 August 2006.

Scan this QR code with your smart device to watch Theo use his blistering pace to rip Scotland apart and score in August 2013 on the official England YouTube channel, FA TV.

FATV

38 CAPS

7 ASSISTS

OFF THE PITCH
Theo enjoys golf, has written four story books for children and liked maths at school. His favourite biscuit is a digestive!

THEO'S SPRINT TIPS:

"The most important thing is to start low. When I push off, I'm very low and my head's down and my power is generated from my legs."

5 GOALS FOR ENGLAND

1 SCORED AT HOME

4 SCORED AWAY

THREE-0 WALCOTT!

Theo is the only player in the current squad ever to have scored a hat-trick, which he netted against Croatia in September 2008.

"IF WE LOOK AFTER EACH OTHER, BELIEVE IN EACH OTHER, WHICH IS IMPORTANT TO ME, I THINK WE CAN GO FAR."

BURSTING CLEAR!

As the ball is played downfield, Theo starts his run. Normally he's great at timing, but this time he's only onside once. Can you spot in which picture he's beaten the offside trap?

A   **B**   **C**   **D**

Answer: C

59

HOW TO PLAY LIKE AN
ENGLAND STAR

FATV

If you want to be an England star, you'll have to learn to play like one! The skills you'll learn about on this page will help you take your game to the next level and impress your friends. Who knows one day it could you pulling on that number 10 shirt instead of Wayne Rooney!

HOW TO MAKE GREAT SAVES!

GOALKEEPING

When you are saving the ball it is important to think about how you land so you don't get hurt. It's best to put your weight on your thigh and your shoulder. Make sure you have one hand behind the ball and one hand on top of it. Scan this code to see the England goalies train!

HOW TO RUSH OFF THE LINE!

GOALKEEPING

The first step is to close the space down, keeping your eye on the ball but checking your position in the goal. Then burst forward but don't get too close to the ball in case you get chipped by the attacker. Bend your knees slightly, stay on your toes and keep the palms of your hands facing out. Make yourself as big as you can and don't commit yourself to the dive. Scan this QR code with your smart device to see Joe Hart show how to come off your line against Peru.

HOW TO BLOCK SHOTS

DEFENDING

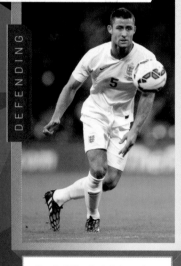

HOW TO TAKE THE PERFECT CORNER!

TARGETING

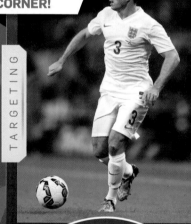

HOW TO CLOSE DOWN

DEFENDING

The first thing to do is to work out which way the attacker is going. With your back to goal try to guide them where you want them to go. It's important to get yourself between the ball and the goal. Don't get too close or they might sell you a dummy. Then get your body in the way and block the shot. Scan this code to watch Gary Cahill's block against Poland.

There are two types of corner: the near post corner and the far post corner. For both, place your non-kicking foot beside or a little bit behind the ball and kick through by striking underneath the ball. It's important to get right under the ball and lean back to give it height. Then watch your striker head it in! Watch Leighton Baines deliver two perfect corners against Peru, which both led to England goals, by scanning this code.

Cover the space where you think the ball will be played and run towards the player with ball and face him by standing side on with your knees bent. When closing down, it is important to run as quickly as possible at first to close down the space and then slow down as you approach the player, so he doesn't trick you. Scan this QR code to see how Phil Jagielka anticipates where the ball is going and closes down the space in front of his attacker against Italy.

HOW TO MAKE A KILLER PASS

PASSING

The killer pass happens when you play the ball between two defenders and the attacker gets the ball the other side and scores! If you can't play it through straight away, be patient and wait for the right moment before attempting your defence-splitting pass! Scan this QR code to watch Jack Wilshere's killer passes against Brazil.

HOW TO VOLLEY!

SHOOTING

The key with volleying is to keep your eye on the ball. You can use the laces part of your boot or your instep. Try to shape your body to make a good contact, keeping your head and knee over the ball, and then place it past the keeper. Goooaaaal! Scan this QR code to watch Alex Oxlade-Chamberlain's volley against Brazil.

HOW TO PASS WITH BOTH FEET

PASSING

This drill is a good way of getting used to using both feet. Place your non-kicking foot next to the ball and use the inside of your right foot to play the ball in a short pass to your team-mate, who controls it and passes it back to you. Now when you receive the ball, pull it across with your right foot and play it with your left foot. Then try it the other way round. Adam Lallana is very two-footed. Scan this QR code to watch Adam's masterclass on how to improve your weaker foot.

HOW TO DODGE A MAN MARKER!

MOVEMENT

Take two small steps to one side to trick your marker into thinking you are going to run that way, then quickly move back into the space you've left behind you and call for the ball. If the defender comes with you, you will have to make a second movement into another space to shake him off before you can receive the ball. Scan this QR code to see how Raheem Sterling loses his marker to score against Lithuania. Also note Danny Welbeck's decoy run!

HOW TO SCORE A PENALTY

SHOOTING

You don't need a long run-up to take a great penalty. Take a few steps back, place your non-kicking foot by the ball and with your toe pointing down, strike the ball with the laces part of your boot. Try to aim for the corners, keep your knee over ball, follow through and you'll beat the keeper! Scan this QR code to watch Wayne Rooney's clinical penalty technique against Norway.

FOR EVEN MORE SKILLS, HEAD TO THE FA SKILLS WEBSITE AT

MIDFIELDER

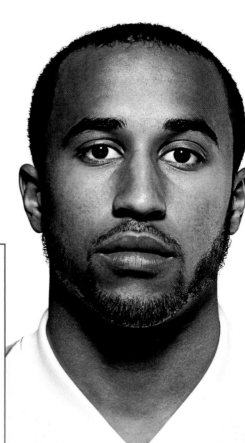

ANDROS HAS SCORED IN 43% OF HIS ENGLAND GAMES!

ANDROS TOWNSEND

USUAL SHIRT NUMBER

TOWNSEND
7

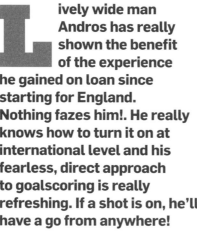

Lively wide man Andros has really shown the benefit of the experience he gained on loan since starting for England. Nothing fazes him!. He really knows how to turn it on at international level and his fearless, direct approach to goalscoring is really refreshing. If a shot is on, he'll have a go from anywhere!

D.O.B. 16/07/91
Height: 1.81m
Weight: 81kg

PLACE OF BIRTH
Leytonstone, London
Leytonstone is 237km (147 miles) from St George's Park but it's only 33km (21 miles) from Wembley! Just a run down the wing!

HOME BOY
While the average player has to travel almost exactly 1000 miles for each of their England appearances (1001), Andros has only had to travel an average of **82 miles** for each of his! The friendly with Italy in March was the only one of his seven appearances not to have been staged at Wembley.

HOT SHOT
ANDROS HAS SHOT MORE REGULARLY THAN ANY CURRENT MIDFIELDER: 3.27 TIMES PER MATCH OR ONCE EVERY 27 MINUTES 32 SECONDS.

Domestic clubs:
Tottenham Hotspur (2008-present)
Yeovil Town (Mar-Jun 2009 loan)
Leyton Orient (Aug 2009-Jan 2010 loan)
MK Dons (Jan-Feb 2010 loan)
Ipswich Town (Aug-Dec 2010 loan)
Watford (Jan-Feb 2011 loan)
Millwall (Mar-May 2011 loan)
Leeds United (Jan-Feb 2012 loan)
Birmingham City (Feb-May 2012 loan)
QPR (Jan-May 2013 loan)

LOAN RANGER!
Andros has been loaned to nine different teams in his career, but he's looking like he's here to stay with England!

ENGLAND DEBUT
11/10/13 MONTENEGRO (H) 4-1

Although a surprise selection, Andros capped a dream debut with a spectacular, swerving strike after 78 minutes.

3
ALL THREE OF HIS GOALS HAVE COME IN THE SECOND HALF OF ENGLAND MATCHES!

@andros_townsend

289K Followers on Twitter

ANDROS IS BOSS!

Scan this QR code with your smart device to watch Andros' equalising thunderbolt against Italy in March 2015 on the official England YouTube channel, FA TV

FATV

DREAM DEBUT!

"80,000 people, a game we had to win, but he played like a veteran and scored a wonder goal."

England manager Roy Hodgson's praise for Andros after his first game against Montenegro.

On as a 70th-minute sub for Fabian Delph, Andros came to England's rescue with a rising long-range piledriver than earnt England a draw in this friendly. Go Andros!

ON THE BREAK!

This player likes to play on the break. Can you tell who it is slicing through the defence?

Answer: Alex Oxlade-Chamberlain

7 CAPS

OFF THE PITCH

Andros is a big fan of darts, enjoys playing FIFA and is very close to his father, Troy, who has helped his career massively.

MIDFIELDER
(Left-footed)

Quick and great with the ball at his feet, Andros injects urgency into the team.

HEAT MAP

England's options:

Page 48   Page 50   Page 54

POSITION

ANDROS HAS HIT THE WOODWORK TWICE WHILE PLAYING FOR ENGLAND!

ANDROS HAS PLAYED IN FRONT OF THE HIGHEST AVERAGE ATTENDANCE OF ANY CURRENT ENGLAND PLAYER: 67,654!

FORWARD

USUAL SHIRT NUMBER

STURRIDGE
9

16 CAPS

DANIEL STURRIDGE

Daniel has really blossomed as a striker at Liverpool. Tricky and pacy, he is now one of England's top goalscorers. He can hit long-range 'worldies', and is also nearly always in the right place at the right time as his close-range goal against Italy in the 2014 World Cup proved.

D.O.B. 01/09/89

Height: 1.88m

Weight: 76kg

PLACE OF BIRTH

Birmingham
Birmingham is 55km (34 miles) from St George's Park but it's 196km (122 miles) from England's home Wembley. Daniel dances all the way!

ENGLAND DEBUT
15/11/11 SWEDEN (H) 1-0

Daniel came on as a 58th-minute sub for Theo Walcott in England's 1-0 home friendly win.

Domestic clubs:
Liverpool
(2013-present)
Bolton Wanderers
(Jan-May 2011 loan)
Chelsea
(2009-13)
Manchester City
(2006-09)

DANIEL WEARS
NIKE HYPERVENOM

1.52m
Followers on Twitter

@D_Sturridge

64

5 GOALS

FOX IN THE BOX!

THREE OF DANIEL'S FIVE GOALS HAVE COME IN THE SIX-YARD BOX. HE ALSO HAS 100% PENALTY RECORD FOR ENGLAND: ONE OUT OF ONE!

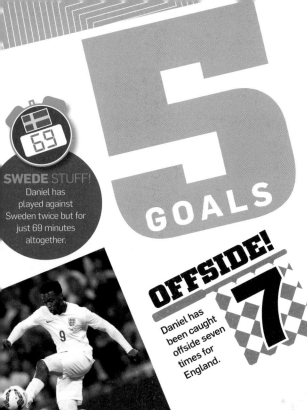

SWEDE STUFF!
Daniel has played against Sweden twice but for just 69 minutes altogether.

OFFSIDE! 7
Daniel has been caught offside seven times for England.

Whether right at the start of a match or as a sub, Daniel likes to come onto the pitch, **BACKWARDS!**

POSITION

FORWARD
(Left-footed)
Daniel's fabulous footwork often leaves defenders trailing in his wake!

HEAT MAP

England's options:

Page 66   Page 70   Page 72

1 ASSIST

1 GOAL

2 GOALS

2 GOALS

Daniel has scored two goals with his left foot, two headers and one with his right for England... so far!

DANCING DANIEL!

There's only one Daniel Sturridge, except... er... here there are two! Can you spot the five differences we've made to Daniel's celebration?

Scan this QR code with your smart device to listen to Daniel talking about the early part of his career on the official England YouTube channel, FA TV.

FATV

Answers: Pigeon, bowling ball, Harry Kane, number on shorts and boots.

 65

FORWARD

DANNY WELBECK

USUAL SHIRT NUMBER

WELBECK
9

Scoring in more than one in three of his England games, Danny is a great finisher with a hard-working attitude to match. A real athlete and a great team player he usually plays as a striker but his pace is also a useful asset in wide areas. More goals are definitely on the cards for the Arsenal star.

PLACE OF BIRTH

Manchester
Manchester is 118km (73 miles) from St George's Park but it's a long 315km (196 miles) from Wembley! Go for the burn, Danny!

Domestic clubs:
Arsenal
(2014-present)
Sunderland
(Aug 2010-May 2011 loan)
Preston North End
(Jan-Jun 2010 loan)
Manchester United
(2007-14)

D.O.B. 26/11/90
Height: 1.85m
Weight: 73kg

33
CAPS

ENGLAND DEBUT 29/03/11 GHANA (H) 1-1

Then a Manchester United player (on loan at Sunderland), Danny came on for Ashley Young after 81 minutes in this friendly.

2180
TOTAL MINS PLAYED

DANNY WEARS
NIKE HYPERVENOM

FORWARD
(Right-footed)

With a superb strike-rate, pace and power, Danny spearheads England's attack.

HEAT MAP

England's options:

Page 64 · Page 70 · Page 72

POSITION

MANNEQUIN MAZE

The England training team have set Danny an interesting challenge. Can he dribble out of this mannequin maze without getting lost? He needs your help guys!

START

FINISH

DEADLY DANNY!

1 HEAD
8 RIGHT FOOT
5 LEFT FOOT

Of Danny's 14 England goals, eight have been struck with his right foot, five with his left and one header! He's also hit the woodwork twice!

CANNY DANNY
One of Danny's cleverest goals came in a 3-2 win over Sweden at Euro 2012 as he backheel-volleyed a winner to give England their first competitive victory over the Swedes.

14 GOALS

ENGLAND HAVE SCORED **52** GOALS WHILE DANNY HAS BEEN PLAYING.

"I'VE GOT VERY HIGH EXPECTATIONS OF MYSELF AND I KNOW WHAT I'M CAPABLE OF AND WHAT I CAN ACHIEVE."

NICKNAME: **DAT GUY!**

Scan this QR code with your smart device to watch Danny's two goals as England came back to beat Slovenia 3-1 in November 2014 on the official England YouTube channel, FA TV.

FATV

LIONESSES

T en out of ten in World Cup qualifying is a record to be extremely proud of! Mark Sampson's side rounded off their brilliant campaign with a 10-0 win over Montenegro. After a couple of friendlies in the build-up to the 2015 World Cup, England's Lionesses were all set to roar in Canada!

KAREN
BARDSLEY
1
GOALKEEPER
14/10/84
1.81m
44 CAPS
Manchester City WFC

ALEX
SCOTT
2
RIGHT-BACK
14/10/84
1.63m
123 CAPS
Arsenal Ladies FC

CLAIRE
RAFFERTY
3
LEFT-BACK
11/01/89
1.61m
10 CAPS
Chelsea LFC

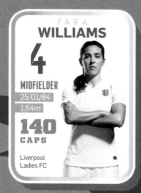

FARA
WILLIAMS
4
MIDFIELDER
25/01/84
1.64m
140 CAPS
Liverpool Ladies FC

STEPHANIE
HOUGHTON
5
CENTRE-BACK
23/04/88
1.72m
54 CAPS
Manchester City WFC
CAPTAIN

LAURA
BASSETT
6
CENTRE-BACK
02/08/83
1.66m
49 CAPS
Notts County LFC

JORDAN
NOBBS
7
MIDFIELDER
08/12/92
1.60m
21 CAPS
Arsenal Ladies FC

JILL
SCOTT
8
MIDFIELDER
02/02/87
1.80m
91 CAPS
Manchester City WFC

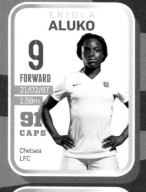

ENIOLA
ALUKO
9
FORWARD
21/02/87
1.58m
91 CAPS
Chelsea LFC

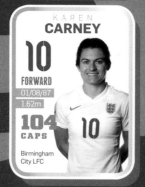

KAREN
CARNEY
10
FORWARD
01/08/87
1.62m
104 CAPS
Birmingham City LFC

JADE
MOORE
11
MIDFIELDER
22/10/90
1.65m
17 CAPS
Birmingham City LFC

LUCY
BRONZE
12
RIGHT-BACK
28/10/91
1.73m
17 CAPS
Manchester City WFC

SIOBHAN
CHAMBERLAIN
13
GOALKEEPER
15/08/83
1.80m
33 CAPS
Arsenal Ladies FC

ALEX
GREENWOOD
14
LEFT-BACK
07/09/93
1.68m
13 CAPS
Notts County LFC

CASEY
STONEY
15
DEFENDER
13/05/82
1.72m
119 CAPS
Arsenal Ladies FC

KATIE
CHAPMAN
16
MIDFIELDER
15/06/82
1.70m
86 CAPS
Chelsea LFC

JO
POTTER
17
MIDFIELDER
13/11/84
1.74m
19 CAPS
Birmingham City LFC

TONI
DUGGAN
18
FORWARD
25/07/91
1.67m
26 CAPS
Manchester City WFC

JODIE
TAYLOR
19
FORWARD
17/05/86
1.63m
8 CAPS
Portland Thorns (USA)

LIANNE
SANDERSON
20
FORWARD
03/02/88
1.68m
47 CAPS
Arsenal Ladies FC

CARLY
TELFORD
21
GOALKEEPER
07/07/87
1.72m
6 CAPS
Notts County LFC

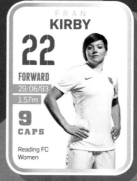

FRAN
KIRBY
22
FORWARD
29/06/93
1.57m
9 CAPS
Reading FC Women

ELLEN
WHITE
23
FORWARD
09/05/89
1.71m
51 CAPS
Notts County LFC

IN THE GAME WITH EA SPORTS FIFA 16

You've only got to look at the stars of the England women's team on the opposite page to see how far women's football has come in England in the last few years. Crowds are up: in November 2014, 50,000 fans saw the Lionesses play a friendly against Germany at Wembley. Football is now one of the largest female participation sports in England, there is a professional league and the BBC showed all 52 matches at the World Cup. And if that wasn't enough, the Lionesses are now 'In The Game'!

Players will perform exactly as they do on the pitch.

Yes, for the first time ever, the 12 top-ranked women's national teams, which of course include England, are appearing in EA SPORTS™ FIFA 16. How cool is that? So as well as England, you will also be able to play with these 11 other teams:

- Australia
- Brazil
- Canada
- China
- France
- Germany
- Italy
- Mexico
- Spain
- Sweden
- USA

But we know you'll want to try England first!

"It's a great opportunity for the girls to be involved. It shows how far women's football has come!" - Steph

As usual EA have done an absolutely awesome job of recreating the look and movements of every single player and all the women's national teams look so brilliantly lifelike, you could almost mistake them for the real thing!

Mark Sampson's Lionesses are thrilled to be part of FIFA 16 and are looking forward having a go at playing as England in FIFA 16. England captain, Stephanie Houghton said: "To find out we will be included in FIFA for the first time is a special feeling. Featuring on FIFA is new to the women's game and raises awareness of the game to a new audience."

This is a great step forward for the women's game. Football is everyone's game and now everyone's 'In The Game'!

To hear how thrilled the Lionesses are to be included in FIFA 16 scan this QR code with your smart device:

A mobile headscanning unit scans Eniola Aluko's face to capture each feature.

Every facial feature is recorded including hairstyles.

WIN AN XBOX ONE AND COPIES OF FIFA 16!

To celebrate England's women being included in FIFA 16, we are offering a brilliant prize giveaway! There are two Xbox Ones both with a copy of the game and six individual copies of FIFA 16 up for grabs! To enter our prize draws, answer this question:

WHICH LIONESS WAS THE SQUAD CAPTAIN FOR THE FIFA 2015 WOMEN'S WORLD CUP?

A) LUCY BRONZE   B) JILL SCOTT   C) STEPHANIE HOUGHTON

Send your answer to us via email to: eafifa16@paninicomps.co.uk
Write FIFA 16 COMPETITION in the subject bar of your email.
Make sure you tell us your name, age and address in your email!

CLOSING DATES:
The first draw will be on the 4th JANUARY 2016 for an XBOX ONE and a copy of the game and three further lucky winners will receive a copy of FIFA 16. The second draw will be on the 2nd MAY 2016 for an XBOX ONE and a copy of the game and three further lucky winners will receive a copy of FIFA 16.

COMPETITION RULES:
See above for how to enter by email.
The promoter is Panini UK Ltd. Brockbourne House, 77 Mount Ephraim, Tunbridge Wells TN4 8BS. Make sure we have your entry before the final draw on **2nd May 2016**. Please note – If you are a winner in the **4th January 2016** draw you will not be entered into the draw on the **2nd May 2016**. If you are not a winner in the draw on the **4th January 2016** you will automatically be entered into the draw on the **2nd May 2016**. Please ensure you have your parents' consent before entering this competition.
1. You can enter if you live in England, Scotland, Wales, Northern Ireland or the Channel Islands, unless someone in your house is employed by Panini UK Ltd, or EA Sports.
2. By entering this competition, you promise to us that you have read these rules and that you will follow them. 3. We can't allow entries which arrive too late and we can't accept responsibility if your entry is lost. 4. We will choose the winners at random from all the correct answers we receive. 5. One entry per household. We don't allow bulk entries or entries made by other people on your behalf.
We will disqualify all entries which break this rule. 6. If you win, you will receive the prize described. We won't swap the prize for cash. If there is ever a reason why we can't give you exactly the same prize, we will give you something just as good or even better instead. 7. Winners will be contacted within 28 days of the competition closing date, either by post or email. Prize fulfillment will be within 28 days from the date we receive the winners' address details. 8. If we contact you to tell you you're a winner, but you don't reply within a month, we may have to offer the prize to a runner-up, or give it away in a future competition. Your details: we will use your name, address, and any other details that you give us to run this competition. If you win, we will pass them to the person who is providing the prize so that they can post it to you, we won't provide them to anyone else without your permission. You can find out the winners' first names and county once the competition is over by sending a stamped address envelope to Competition Rules, ATTN., Nick Clark, FIFA 16, Panini UK Ltd., Brockbourne House, 77 Mount Ephraim, Tunbridge Wells, TN4 8BS.

FORWARD

ROONEY
10

England's skipper and top scorer Wayne burst into pro football when he was just 16 at Everton in 2002. He is an amazing talent and a real leader who tries really hard to win every game. At the moment he is third in the list of all-time England goalscorers with 47 goals, but he's defo gonna be No.1!

ENGLAND DEBUT
12/02/03 AUSTRALIA (H) 1-3

Substitute Wayne was England's youngest ever player (17 and 111 days), until 2006 when Theo Walcott beat him by being 36 days younger!

WAYNE
ROONEY

@waynerooney

11.2m
Followers on Twitter

ENGLAND STRIKE RATE
0.53
GOALS PER GAME

DID YOU KNOW?

Wayne's heroes when he was a boy were Everton striker Duncan Ferguson and Argentina legend Diego Maradona.

D.O.B. 24/10/85

Height: 1.78m

Weight: 78kg

Domestic clubs:
Manchester United (2004-present)
Everton (2002-04)

PLACE OF BIRTH

Croxteth, Liverpool
Croxteth is 136km (85 miles) from St George's Park but it's a whole 346km (215 miles) from Wembley. One long training run!

TWO GOOD!

$2 \times 10 = 20$ ✓
$3 \times 0 = 0$ ✗

Wayne has scored two goals for England in **TEN** different games, but hasn't bagged a hat-trick. YET!

ROONEY ROOLS!

Wayne netted his first England goal in a 2-1 away win v. Macedonia in September 2003, making him England's youngest-ever goalscorer.

8019 TOTAL MINS PLAYED

5 DAYS
13 HOURS
39 MINUTES

TIKI-TOKA!

Wayne has racked up 8019 minutes (5 days, 13 hours and 39 minutes) in an England shirt. That's enough time for you to walk from London to Glasgow!

SPOT ON!

4/4

Wayne has scored all four penalties he's taken for England!

40 GOALS

OFF THE PITCH

Wayne is a big boxing fan, enjoys golf, playing Xbox and walking his dogs.

POSITION

FORWARD
(Right-footed)

Wayne can lead the line or play as a classic No.10. He is the complete striker!

HEAT MAP

England's options:

| Page 64 | Page 66 | Page 74 |

Wayne is currently the most capped player in the England squad with **50** more than anyone else!

103 CAPS

Scan this QR code to hear Wayne talking about reaching 100 caps for England on the official England YouTube channel, FA TV.

FATV

CAPTAIN

NICKNAME
WAZZA

Can you complete Wayne's World? Choose the correct piece to complete the scene.

?

PUZZLE IT OUT

A
B
C
D

"AS A KID I ALWAYS **LOVED** WATCHING ENGLAND ON THE TELEVISION ... TO BE **CAPTAIN** IS BEYOND MY WILDEST **DREAMS.**"

WAYNE WEARS
NIKE HYPERVENOM

Answer: D

FORWARD

LAMBERT
18

Rickie has come up the hard way. From being released by Liverpool aged 15, he has climbed his way back to the top with both the Reds and England via the lower leagues. A clever striker with superb touch and vision, his debut England goal was the crowning moment of a fairytale comeback.

D.O.B. 16/02/82

Height: 1.88m

Weight: 77kg

PLACE OF BIRTH

Kirkby, Merseyside
Kirkby is 137km (85 miles) from St George's Park but it's much further, 215km (346 miles), to Wembley! See you there, Rickie!

ENGLAND DEBUT 14/08/13 SCOTLAND (H) 3-2

All Rickie's dreams came true on his debut after he stepped off the bench to replace Wayne Rooney and three minutes later headed the winner!

RICKIE

LAMBERT

POSITION

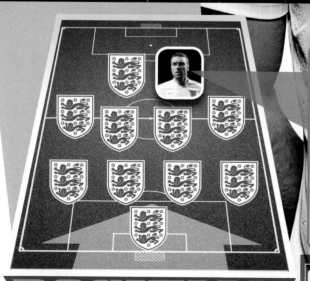

FORWARD
(Right-footed)

Rickie is blessed with touch, a ferocious shot and is great in the air.

HEAT MAP

"IT WAS AMAZING! I COULDN'T HAVE DREAMT FOR IT TO HAVE GONE ANY BETTER, SO I'M OVER THE MOON!"

Rickie on his debut England goal.

Domestic clubs:
Liverpool (2014-present)
Southampton (2009-14)
Bristol Rovers (2006-09)
Rochdale (2005-06)
Stockport (2002-05)
Macclesfield (2001-02)
Blackpool (1998-2000)

England's options:

Page 66   Page 70   Page 74

11 CAPS

4 ASSISTS

72

568,280

FANS HAVE SEEN RICKIE IN ENGLAND ACTION

NICKNAME:

LAMBO!

RICKIE'S ROCKET!

Rickie's third goal for England came in a 2-2 draw with Ecuador in a World Cup warm-up game in June 2014. It was a beautifully hit, drilled right foot shot that gave the keeper no chance.

DID YOU KNOW?

Rickie once worked at a beetroot factory when he didn't have a club. He was paid £20 a day to attach lids to jars!

3 GOALS

HEADERS
2

RIGHT
FOOT
1

100% SCORING RECORD

After his first two games as he hit the net against both Scotland and Moldova.

Scan this QR code with your smart device to watch Rickie climb the highest to head England to victory over Scotland on his debut in August 2013 on the official England YouTube channel, FA TV.

FATV

8

Eight of Rickie's appearances have been as a substitute.

RICKIE'S RIDDLE

Take the first letter of players' No.1 and No.3's first names and add the first letter of player No.2 and No.4's surnames and mix up and what word have you got? Write your answer in the box below.

1
2
3
4

DID YOU KNOW?

FELLOW ENGLAND STAR CALUM CHAMBERS USED TO CLEAN RICKIE'S BOOTS WHEN THEY WERE AT SOUTHAMPTON TOGETHER!

RICKIE HAS PLAYED

259

MINUTES FOR ENGLAND.

....

Answer: Goal

73

FORWARD

USUAL SHIRT NUMBER

CHAMBERLAIN
20

DID YOU KNOW?
Alex's dad, Mark Chamberlain, played for England eight times in the 1980s. He was part of the last England team to win in Brazil in 1984.

With electrifying acceleration and a ton of tricks up his sleeve, Alex plays with a fearless freedom that sets fans' pulses racing. A skilful player with an eye for goal, the Arsenal flyer plays his football with a smile on his face and always brings that something extra to turn matches and unlock defences.

PLACE OF BIRTH

Portsmouth
Portsmouth is 283km (176 miles) from St George's Park but it's much further, 138km (86 miles), to Wembley! Way to go, Alex!

D.O.B. 15/08/93

Height: 1.80m

Weight: 70kg

Domestic clubs:
Arsenal (2011-present)
Southampton (2010 - 11)

ALEX
OXLADE-
CHAMBERLAIN

@Alex_OxChambo

1.89M
Followers on Twitter

Alex always puts his left shinpad on before his right and when he goes out onto the pitch, he take three hops on his left leg!

ENGLAND DEBUT

26/05/12
NORWAY (A) 0-1

Alex came on in the 73rd minute to replace goalscorer Ashley Young as England recorded their first win over Norway for 32 years in Roy Hodgson's first game as manager.

ALEX WEARS
NIKE HYPERVENOM

ENGLAND HAVE SCORED IN EVERY MATCH ALEX HAS PLAYED IN!

FORWARD
(Right footed)

Alex is the kind of lively striker defenders hate and always makes things happen.

HEAT MAP

England's options:

Page 64 | Page 66 | Page 72

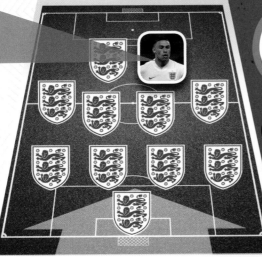

POSITION

NICKNAME
THE OX

TWENTY-ONE

OF ALEX'S 25 ATTEMPTS ON GOAL HAVE BEEN WITH HIS RIGHT-FOOT.

Scan this QR code with your smart device to enjoy Alex's first ever England goal in a 5-0 home win over San Marino in October 2012 on the official England YouTube channel, FA TV.

FATV

ENGLAND HAVE KEPT **CLEAN SHEETS** IN **HALF** OF ALEX'S MATCHES.

4 GOALS

The Ox celebrates scoring his opener against Scotland.

20 CAPS

NAME FAME

ALEXANDER OXLADE-CHAMBERLAIN

TOTAL 26

Alex has the longest name (leaving middle names out) of any player to have played for England!

BRAZIL BELTER!

It's always special to score against Brazil and Alex came off the bench to fire England ahead with a sweet volley in the Maracana Stadium in June 2013. The game ended as a 2-2 draw.

PICTURE PUZZLE

This one's easy. All you've got to do is work out which picture links to which England player? Answers below.

ANSWER: 1. Joe HART 2. Alex 'THE OX' Oxlade-Chamberlain 3. Kyle WALKER 4. Raheem STERLING.

 75

TOP PICKS

GOALKEEPER

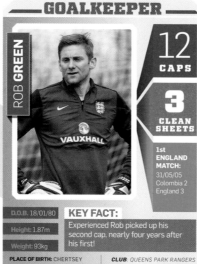

ROB GREEN

12 CAPS

3 CLEAN SHEETS

1st ENGLAND MATCH:
31/05/05
Colombia 2
England 3

D.O.B. 18/01/80
Height: 1.87m
Weight: 93kg

KEY FACT:
Experienced Rob picked up his second cap, nearly four years after his first!

PLACE OF BIRTH: CHERTSEY | CLUB: QUEENS PARK RANGERS

GOALKEEPER

JACK BUTLAND

1 CAP

2 SAVES

1st ENGLAND MATCH:
15/08/12
England 2
Italy 1

D.O.B. 10/03/93
Height: 1.92m
Weight: 95kg

KEY FACT:
Agile Jack played a starring role for Team GB in the London 2012 Olympics.

PLACE OF BIRTH: BRISTOL | CLUB: STOKE CITY

GOALKEEPER

TOM HEATON

3 UNDER-21s CAPS

1 UNDER-21s CLEAN SHEETS

1st ENGLAND UNDER-21s MATCH:
25/03/08
England 0
Poland 0

D.O.B. 15/04/86
Height: 1.88m
Weight: 85kg

KEY FACT:
Tom is the first Burnley player in 40 years to be called up for the England senior team!

PLACE OF BIRTH: CHESTER | CLUB: BURNLEY

LEFT-BACK

KIERAN GIBBS

7 CAPS

1 CLEAN SHEET

1st ENGLAND MATCH:
11/08/10
England 2
Hungary 1

D.O.B. 26/09/89
Height: 1.78m
Weight: 70kg

KEY FACT:
Reliable Kieran came on at half-time for Ashley Cole in his first England game.

PLACE OF BIRTH: LAMBETH, LONDON | CLUB: ARSENAL

DEFENDER

CALUM CHAMBERS

3 CAPS

3 CLEAN SHEETS

1st ENGLAND MATCH:
03/09/14
England 1
Norway 0

D.O.B. 20/01/95
Height: 1.83m
Weight: 66kg

KEY FACT:
One of England's most promising young defenders, Calum is versatile too!

PLACE OF BIRTH: PETERSFIELD | CLUB: ARSENAL

LEFT-BACK

DANNY ROSE

29 UNDER-21s CAPS

3 UNDER-21s GOALS

1st ENGLAND UNDER-21s MATCH:
08/06/09
England 7
Azerbaijan 0

D.O.B. 02/07/90
Height: 1.73m
Weight: 72kg

KEY FACT:
Danny got his first call up to the England squad in September 2014.

PLACE OF BIRTH: DONCASTER | CLUB: TOTTENHAM HOTSPUR

LEFT-BACK

RYAN BERTRAND

3 CAPS

1 MATCHES WON

1st ENGLAND MATCH:
15/08/12
England 2
Italy 1

D.O.B. 05/08/89
Height: 1.79m
Weight: 85kg

KEY FACT:
Ryan has played for England at U17, U18, U19, U20, Under-21 and senior levels!

PLACE OF BIRTH: SOUTHWARK, LONDON | CLUB: SOUTHAMPTON

DEFENDER

JOHN STONES

4 CAPS

3 CLEAN SHEETS

1st ENGLAND MATCH:
30/05/14
England 3
Peru 0

D.O.B. 28/05/94
Height: 1.88m
Weight: 70kg

KEY FACT:
John shows great composure for a young player and has a big England future ahead of him.

PLACE OF BIRTH: HEMSWORTH | CLUB: EVERTON

Here are some of the other key players ready to leap into action as soon as Roy says the word!

MIDFIELDER

JONJO SHELVEY

1 CAP

1 MATCH WON

1st ENGLAND MATCH:
12/10/12
England 5
San Marino 0

D.O.B. 27/02/92
Height: 1.74m
Weight: 78kg

KEY FACT:
Jonjo loves to shoot from range and got two shots in on his only England start to date.

PLACE OF BIRTH: ROMFORD,LONDON   **CLUB:** SWANSEA CITY

MIDFIELDER

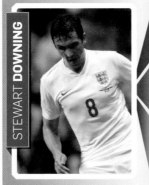

STEWART DOWNING

35 CAPS

7 ASSISTS

1st ENGLAND MATCH:
09/02/05
England 0
Holland 0

D.O.B. 22/07/84
Height: 1.80m
Weight: 64kg

KEY FACT:
His excellent form for West Ham earned Stewart a recall to the England squad in November 2014.

PLACE OF BIRTH: MIDDLESBROUGH   **CLUB:** WEST HAM UNITED

MIDFIELDER

MICHAEL CARRICK

33 CAPS

1 ASSIST

1st ENGLAND MATCH:
25/05/01
England 4
Mexico 0

D.O.B. 28/07/81
Height: 1.88m
Weight: 74kg

KEY FACT:
A fabulous passer, Michael is also great at screening his centre-backs.

PLACE OF BIRTH: WALLSEND   **CLUB:** MANCHESTER UNITED

MIDFIELDER

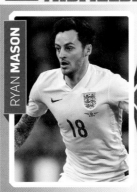

RYAN MASON

1 CAP

1 ASSIST

1st ENGLAND MATCH:
31/03/15
Italy 1
England 1

D.O.B. 13/06/91
Height: 1.75m
Weight: 68kg

KEY FACT:
Ryan provided the assist for Andros Townsend's equaliser in his first England game.

PLACE OF BIRTH: ENFIELD   **CLUB:** TOTTENHAM HOTSPUR

MIDFIELDER

FABIAN DELPH

5 CAPS

4 CLEAN SHEETS

1st ENGLAND MATCH:
03/09/14
England 1
Norway 0

D.O.B. 21/11/89
Height: 1.74m
Weight: 60kg

KEY FACT:
All-action midfielder Fabian's form for Aston Villa saw him force his way into the England team.

PLACE OF BIRTH: BRADFORD   **CLUB:** ASTON VILLA

FORWARD

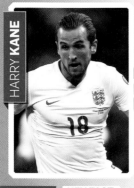

HARRY KANE

2 CAPS

1 GOAL

1st ENGLAND MATCH:
27/03/15
England 4
Lithuania 0

D.O.B. 28/07/93
Height: 1.83m
Weight: 65kg

KEY FACT:
Talk about making a splash! Harry scored for England after only 79 seconds on the pitch on his debut!

PLACE OF BIRTH: CHINGFORD   **CLUB:** TOTTENHAM HOTSPUR

FORWARD

CHARLIE AUSTIN

D.O.B. 05/07/89
Height: 1.88m
Weight: 84kg

KEY FACT:
While playing for non-league Poole Town, Charlie worked as a bricklayer!

PLACE OF BIRTH: HUNGERFORD   **CLUB:** QUEENS PARK RANGERS

FORWARD

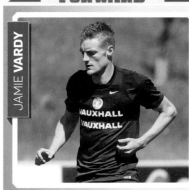

JAMIE VARDY

D.O.B. 11/01/87
Height: 1.78m
Weight: 76kg

KEY FACT:
Jamie scored a hatful of goals when playing for non-league Fleetwood Town!

PLACE OF BIRTH: SHEFFIELD   **CLUB:** LEICESTER CITY

THE BIG FAT ENGLAND FOOTY QUIZ

Now you've read the annual and (hopefully enjoyed it!), it's time for your England exam! Only joking, but do have a go at our little England quiz to see how much you really know about the team. Good luck!

HINT: YOU MIGHT FIND SOME OF THE ANSWERS IN THE ANNUAL!

THE MANAGEMENT

1 Who was Roy Hodgson's first match against?

a) Sweden
b) Norway
c) France
d) Italy

2 Who is the England Under-21s manager?
a) Gareth Southgate
b) Alan Curbishley
c) Sean Dyche
d) Alan Shearer

3 Who is the England Women's manager?
a) Kenny Sansom
b) Santi Cazorla
c) Jacqui Oatley
d) Mark Sampson

4 Who was manager when England won the World Cup in 1966?
a) Gordon Ramsay
b) Alf Ramsey
c) Pep Guardiola
d) Gordon Banks

5 Which club did Roy Hodgson and his assistant Ray Lewington work at together?
a) West Ham
b) Notts County
c) Fulham
d) Leeds

THE TEAM

6 Which current England player was born outside England?
a) Adam Lallana
b) Raheem Sterling
c) Daniel Sturridge
d) Phil Jagielka

7 Who is the oldest player ever to play for England?
a) Stanley Matthews
b) David James
c) Leon Osman
d) Matthew Le Tissier

8 Who is the tallest player ever to play for England?
a) Peter Crouch
b) Fraser Forster
c) Jackie Charlton
d) Gary Cahill

9 When was the first England international?
a) 1972
b) 1872
c) 1672
d) 1072

10 How many Euro finals have England played in so far?
a) 2
b) 6
c) 8
d) All of them!

11 When did England host the Euro finals?
a) 1996
b) 1968
c) 2000
d) 1988

12 Which outfield player has the most England caps?

Paul Gascoigne   Paul Scholes
Gary Neville   David Beckham

13 How many England teams are there altogether?
a) 1
b) 16
c) 8
d) 24

14 What is England's highest ever FIFA ranking?
a) 1st
b) 2nd
c) 17th
d) 3rd

THE FACILITIES

15 What is the capacity of Wembley?
a) 79,000
b) 102,000
c) 9
d) 90,000

16 What was the famous feature of the old Wembley?
a) A very tall spire
b) A giant gate
c) Twin towers
d) A huge clock

17 How many toilets are there at Wembley?
a) None
b) 2618
c) 15
d) 350

18 Which county is St George's Park in?
a) Kent
b) Yorkshire
c) Staffordshire
d) Dorset

19 How many full-size football pitches are there at St George's Park?
a) 12
b) 8
c) 43
d) 1

And one for fun!

20 What are the names of England's three lion mascots?
a) Paws, Mayne and Roary
b) Geoff, Bobby and Jack
c) Kevin, Kenny and Keith
d) George, Leo and Rex

WE HOPE YOU DIDN'T FIND THAT TOO HARD. HOW DID YOU GET ON? CHECK THE ANSWERS BELOW AND WRITE YOUR SCORE OUT OF 20 HERE.

RATINGS:
0 – non-league
1-5 – League 2
5-10 – League 1
10-15 - The Championship
15-19 - Premier League
20/20 – England class!

ANSWERS
1 b) Norway
2 a) Gareth Southgate
3 d) Mark Sampson
4 b) Alf Ramsey
5 c) Fulham
6 b) Raheem Sterling
7 a) Sir Stanley Matthews (he was 42!)
8 a) Peter Crouch
9 b) 1872
10 c) 8
11 a) 1996
12 b) David Beckham
13 d) 24
14 d) 3rd
15 d) 90,000
16 c) Twin towers
17 b) 2618
18 c) Staffordshire
19 a) 12
20 a) Paws, Mane and Roary